An Encyclopedia of

BIBLEANIMALS

An Encyclopedia of
BIBLEANIMALS

Peter France
Photographs by Eric and David Hosking

CROOM HELM
London & Sydney

*TO WHOM BETTER THAN THE SOCIETY FOR THE
PROTECTION OF NATURE IN ISRAEL (SPNI) TO DEDICATE
THIS BOOK FOR THEY ARE THE WORTHY GUARDIANS OF
THE 'BIBLE ANIMALS'*

© 1986 Peter France, Eric and David Hosking
Croom Helm Ltd, Provident House, Burrell Row, Beckenham, Kent BR3 1AT
Croom Helm Australia Pty Ltd, Suite 4, 6th Floor, 64–76 Kippax Street,
Surry Hills, NSW 2010, Australia

British Library Cataloguing in Publication Data
France, Peter
   An encyclopedia of Bible animals.
   1. Bible — Natural history
   I. Title   II. Hosking, Eric   III. Hosking, David
220.8′591   BS663

ISBN 0-7099-3737-7

Typeset in Korinna by Columns of Reading
Printed and bound in Great Britain

CONTENTS

Acknowledgements   6
Introduction   7
List of Abbreviations   9
Adder   10
Ant   12
Ape   13
Asp   14
Ass   16
Badger   18
Bat   20
Bear   21
Bee   23
Beetle   25
Behemoth   26
Bittern   28
Boar   30
Camel   31
Cankerworm   33
Caterpillar   34
Cattle   35
Chameleon   37
Chamois   39
Chicken   39
Cock   40
Cockatrice   41
Coney   42
Cormorant   44
Crane   45
Cuckoo   46
Deer   47
Dog   50
Dove   52
Eagle   54
Fallow Deer   57
Ferret   58

Flea   58
Fly   60
Fox   60
Frog   62
Gazelle   64
Gecko   65
Gier   66
Glede   67
Gnat   68
Goat   69
Grasshopper   71
Greyhound   73
Hare   74
Hawk   76
Hen   78
Heron   79
Hoopoe   80
Hornet   82
Horse   83
Horseleach   85
Hyena   86
Ibex   88
Jackal   89
Kite   91
Lapwing   93
Leopard   94
Leviathan   96
Lice   98
Lion   100
Lizard   103
Locust   105
Mole   107
Moth   108
Mouse   110
Mule   112

Night Hawk   113
Osprey   114
Ossifrage   115
Ostrich   117
Owl   118
Palmerworm   120
Partridge   121
Peacock   124
Pelican   125
Pygarg   127
Quail   128
Raven   130
Satyr   132
Scorpion   133
Screech Owl   135
Sheep   136
Snail   138
Sparrow   140
Spider   142
Stork   144
Swallow   145
Swan   147
Swine   148
Tortoise   150
Unicorn   151
Viper   152
Vulture   154
Weasel   156
Whale   158
Wild Ass   159
Wild Goat   161
Wolf   162
Worm   164
Bibliography   166

ACKNOWLEDGEMENTS

It is hardly surprising that the cradle of a great variety of human civilisation should also be the home of a great variety of animal life. However, the Middle East is far from being a wildlife sanctuary and hunting is a popular pastime. Fortunately the Society for the Protection of Nature in Israel (SPNI) has come to the aid of threatened wildlife, making this one of the most conservation-minded countries in the world.

We cannot express sufficiently our thanks to the SPNI, and especially to Yossi Lesham, Ofer Bahat and Reuben Joseph for their help in taking many of the photographs reproduced in this book. Many of the animals mentioned in the Bible may be seen at the Tel-Aviv University Zoo, and Professor Mendelsohn, its creator and inspiration, gave us every assistance to obtain pictures of some of the reptiles and mammals.

There are a host of people we would like to thank, but space permits us to mention only a few. First among these must be our wives, who have helped in so many ways. It was David's wife, Jean, who first had the idea for this book. She now manages the Frank Lane Picture Agency, which supplied a few of the illustrations we were unable to take ourselves.

During 1963, 1965 and 1966 Eric visited Jordan with Guy Mountfort and Duncan Reid and he would like to express his thanks for making these visits possible. It was John Burton and Michael Bright who introduced us to Peter France to whom we would like to express our thanks for writing such an excellent text. His wife, Felicia, supplied some of the line drawings for which we are very grateful.

None of these photographs would have been possible without the right camera, and so we are indebted to Barry Taylor and all the staff at the Olympus Optical Company who supplied the cameras and other equipment. During our visits to Israel their cameras never let us down, working perfectly in the most trying conditions.

We hope this book will help every reader to understand and appreciate the bible animals and realise what an important place they have in our lives. May Israel continue to set an example to every nation of the world in protecting its wildlife for future generations.

Eric and David Hosking

I NTRODUCTION

When the eagle, most majestic of birds, builds her nest, she chooses a site bold and high, scorning overhang protection, visible to all eyes, yet inaccessible on a cliff face or rocky mountain crag. It is a bulky structure of twigs and branches, built to withstand the buffeting winds and yet lined with grasses, ferns, woodrush and fresh greenery to form a soft bed for her young. And when the time comes for them to leave it and venture out, trusting in their own strength, the eaglets huddle together in the warmth and comfort of the nest like children refusing to get out of bed.

So the mother comes and tears at the nest with her beak and talons, destroying the snugness she has created; she forces the young out onto the high rocks; she even tips them off into space and, as they tumble down, their untried wings flapping to keep them aloft, she swoops beneath them and takes them on her back and carries them to safety. Both natural history and folklore combine in this story. And both are necessary to a complete understanding of Deuteronomy 32:11. God weans his people from their resting place and forces them to try their own strength through affliction. He stirs up the nest. He sometimes lets them fall. But His sustaining mercy is always there at the last to carry them to safety.

The image is rich in implications as are so many of the biblical pictures. And yet, because we are not familiar with the land and culture which shaped them, we may miss their full force. Dr Johnson pointed out that 'These illustrations, though they do not immediately rectify the faith or refine the morals of the reader, yet are by no means to be considered superfluous niceties or useless speculations; for they often show some propriety of allusion utterly undiscoverable by readers not skilled in the natural history of the east.'[1]

Many authors have written on the natural history of Bible lands[2], from Pliny and Strabo, Theophrastus, Galen and Herodotus in ancient times to the botanists and zoologists of the nineteenth century, many of whom were flushed with enthusiasm for the natural sciences and sought to identify

1. In his *Life of Thomas Browne*.
2. 'Bible lands' are the regions over which the activities recorded in Holy Scriptures took place.

precisely in zoological nomenclature the species of animals to which the Bible makes reference.

But they sought precision where precision was not intended. With the possible exception of Solomon, who could speak of trees and beasts and fowl and creeping things and fish (1 Kings 4:33), the authors of the books of the Bible were not field naturalists. They were priests, prophets and kings, as much alive to the legends and folk-tales of the natural world as to the careful observation of the way mammals and birds actually behaved. And so their allusions to natural history are generally incidental or symbolic rather than scientific. They often, and this especially in the lists of unclean and clean animals, added the phrase 'after his kind' to the name of an animal to show that they were indicating generality rather than specificity.

So we have to combine, in our attempts to understand the references to the natural world in the Bible, the legends and folklore of the peoples for whom the books were originally written, with the ecology of the land in which they lived. There are linguistic problems which, it must be admitted, have not yet been solved: many of the words which name the animals are not found outside the lists in the canonical books and so there is no help from other contexts to help identify them; some are now known to be mistranslations as, for example, the references to the Mole (*Talpa europaea*) which has never existed in Bible lands; these almost certainly were meant to refer to the Mole Rat (sub-family *Spalacinae*). And we must remember that the books of the Old Testament were written over a thousand years in time and in many different regions. When we realise today that different animals are called by the same name, and the same animals are called by different names in regional dialects, as well as the names of animals changing through time, we can understand the difficulties in identification that remain.

But great progress has been made in our own generation. Three major new translations and three revisions, all based on the very latest scholarship in the Aramaic and Hebrew languages, have appeared. In Israel, an intense interest in the well-being of the endangered species of animal life has led to the setting up of reserves for the animals mentioned in the Bible and to research into their life-styles which throws light on the biblical references. All this new evidence, linguistic, historical, and biological, has helped with the shaping of the entries in this book.

The word 'animal' is used here in its most general sense: that is, any creature that can feel and move. So it includes a wide range of living creatures, from mammals, through birds and reptiles, to insects. From the Sperm Whale to the Gnat. Each entry begins with a survey of the biblical texts in which the animal is found, with a discussion of the significance of those texts; then the translation is dealt with, including any controversies over the exact meaning; this is followed by the place the animal holds in Jewish myth and legend; and then the notions about the animal which were current at the time of the Authorised Version (on which this encyclopedia is based) are treated; and finally the natural history of the animal with its status in Bible lands today.

ABBREVIATIONS

The following editions of the Bible were consulted:

AV   The Authorised, or King James Version of 1611
        (including the Apocrypha)
GNB   The Good News Bible, or Today's English Version of 1976
JB   The Jerusalem Bible in the English version of 1966
NAS   The New American Standard version of 1971
NEB   The New English Bible of 1970
NIV   The New International Version of 1978
RV   The Revised Version of 1885
RAV   The Revised Authorised Version of 1982

ADDER

There are five references, all in the Old Testament, involving four different Hebrew words. *Shephiphon* is used in the first: 'Dan shall be a serpent by the way, an adder in the path, that biteth the horse's heels' (Gen 49:17) and this has been identified as the Horned Viper (*Cerastes cerastes*) most particularly from its habit, as recorded by Canon Tristram, of hiding in the sand, usually in the impress made by a camel's foot, and darting out to bite passing animals. The force of the image here is that Dan, fifth son of Jacob by the concubine Bilhar, should found a tribe that would extend its territory and conquer its enemies by craft and stealth rather than by open warfare. The tribe did indeed become second only to Judah in numbers (Num 1:39).

Ashuv is the word used in Psalms: 'They have sharpened their tongues like a serpent: adders poison is under their lips' (Psa 140:3), and it is interesting that when St Paul quotes this text in Romans (3:13), he uses the greek word *aspis*, an asp. Here the text simply means a poisonous snake.

Tsiphoni is the word used in Proverbs: 'Look thou not upon the wine when it is red ... at the last it biteth like a serpent and stingeth like an adder' (Prov 23:31-2), and there is a marginal note here with the translation 'COCKATRICE' (q.v.).

Pethen is used in two texts, both from Psalms: 'Thou shalt tread upon the lion and the adder: the young lion and the dragon shalt thou trample under feet' (Psa 91:13); and 'they are like the deaf adder that stoppeth her ear: Which will not hearken to the voice of charmers' (Psa 58:4-5). Here most of the modern versions prefer 'cobra' and, indeed, we associate cobras more than any other species with snake charming. As the word was not known in England until 1668, it was not available for the AV translators, but the naturalist Bartholomew records a habit which is relevant to this text:

> The adder aspis, when she is charmed by the enchanter to come out of her den by charms and conjurations, for she hath no will to come out, layeth her one ear to the ground, and stoppeth that other with the tail, and so she heareth not the voice of the charming, nor cometh out to him that charmeth, nor is obedient to his saying.

Although it is a pleasing picture to imagine a snake with its tail pressed firmly against the side of its head, invulnerable to the persuasions of a flute, there is no confirmation of this habit among today's herpetologists and we must assume that this was a habit assumed from Bible reading rather than observed in the field. Snakes are, of course, deaf, though they are very sensitive to the slightest vibrations in the ground, and they respond to the movement of the charmer's pipe rather than to its sound.

The English word for adder comes from the Anglo-Saxon *naedre*, meaning a serpent, and in the Middle English period 'a naedre' was changed into 'an aedre', and so to 'an adder'. The Common Adder (*Vipera berus*) is the most wide-ranging and common of all snakes. It is the same as the VIPER (q.v.).

North African Horned Viper (*Cerastes cerastes*)

'Look thou not upon the wine when it is red . . . at the last it . . . stingeth like an adder.' (Proverbs 23:31-2)

11

A NT

Desert Ant (*Messer barbarus*)

'The ants are a people not strong, yet they prepare their meat in the summer.' (Proverbs 30:25)

Only twice mentioned, but as an example to all of us in the conduct of our lives: 'Go to the ant, thou sluggard; consider her ways and be wise: Which, having no guide, overseer, or ruler, Provideth her meat in the summer, and gathereth her food in the harvest' (Prov 6:6-8) and 'There be four things which are little upon the earth, but they are exceeding wise: The ants are a people not strong, yet they prepare their meat in the summer' (Prov 30:24-5).

The Hebrew word is *Nmala* and there is no dispute about the translation, though there has been controversy about the accuracy of the natural history. In the nineteenth century, when Bible criticism was in its ascendancy and the accuracy of the Holy Scriptures was under attack, critics seized on the fact that the ants known to observers in Northern Europe did not store up food for the winter. Solomon, they said, must have been mistaken. But the accuracy of the Bible has been vindicated by modern naturalists who have pointed out that the species *Atta barbara*, the Black Ant, and *Atta structor*, the Brown Ant, which are common in Bible lands, do in fact store up grain for the winter, and that this was well known to the ancient writers: Hesiod calls the ant 'the Provident' and writes of its habit of storing grain; Horace speaks of its foresight 'not at all ignorant of or unprotected against the future', as does Aesop in the fable of the Ant and the Grasshopper.

APE

Black-faced Vervet Monkey (*Cercopithecus aethiops*)

'For the king·had at sea a navy . . . bringing gold and silver, ivory and apes and peacocks.' (1 Kings 10:22)

There is only one occasion on which apes are mentioned and this is among the cargoes brought by the ships of Solomon from Tharshish: 'Once in three years came the navy of Tharshish, bringing gold and silver, ivory and apes and peacocks' (1 Kings 10:22 and 2 Chron 9:21).

It has to be admitted that the last three items on this list are hard to identify, since they all relate to objects which were exotic to the Hebrews. The word which is translated 'ape' is the Hebrew *kof*, which has generally been accepted by all translators, though no species of ape is found wild in Bible lands. Monkeys, on the other hand, were known in the ancient world and are represented, with long tails, on Assyrian monuments; they were also worshipped in Egypt and are seen on the wall paintings of Egyptian tombs. The AV translators were familiar with both monkeys and apes, which were caught and taught to do tricks for the entertainment of the court. Since apes seemed to enjoy imitating human behaviour (hence the word 'to ape') they were, it was recorded by the naturalist Bartholomew, caught by this behaviour: 'so oft they shoe themselves with shoes that hunters leave in certain places slyly, and be so taken the sooner; for while they would fasten the thong of the shoe, and would put the shoes on their feet, as they see the hunters do, they be oft taken with the hunters ere they may unlace the shoes and be delivered of them'.

Desert Cobra
(*Walterinnesia aegyptia*)

'And the suckling child
shall play on the hole of
the asp.' (Isaiah 11:8)

The poison of the asp is the characteristic which brings it to the pens of the Old Testament writers. The 'very froward generation', who have left the ways of the Lord, are condemned: 'Their wine is the poison of dragons and the cruel venom of asps' (Deut 32:33); and, although the wickedness of the evil man is sweet in his mouth, yet, 'his meat in his bowels is turned, it is the gall of asps within him' (Job 20:14); and, further, though he hath swallowed down riches, yet, at the end, 'he shall suck the poison of asps' (Job 20:16). And in the final times of the peaceable kingdom, one of the signs shall be that 'the suckling child shall play on the hole of the asp' (Isaiah 11:8).

The Hebrew word is *pethen* and it refers to the Egyptian Cobra (*Naja haje*) which is extremely venomous and lives in a hole in the ground. There was a tendency for all poisonous snakes to be classified under the name 'serpent' (q.v.), but the asp was known as the instrument of suicide among the Egyptians. Cleopatra is known to have died in this way, though the reference in Shakespeare to the 'pretty worm of Nilus that kills and pains not', which she took from a basket and applied to her breast and her arm, could hardly be the fully grown Egyptian Cobra, which reaches a length of eight and a half feet.

The AV translators knew of the special place of the asp in Egyptian culture and an instance of this is recorded in the contemporary Topsell's *History of Serpents*:

> In Egypt, so great is the reverence they bear to Asps that if any in the house have need to rise in the night time out of their beds, they first of all give out a sign by knacking of the fingers, lest they should harm the Asp, and so provoke it against them; at the hearing whereof all the Asps get them to their holes and lodgings, till the person stirring be again in his bed.

A note to the writing of the naturalist Bartholomew on this topic points out that: 'Asp's sting is not curable, but only with the water of a stone washed, which they take out of the sepulchre of an ancient king.' The venom is extremely fast acting and works on the nervous system rather than on the blood of the toads and small birds on which the Egyptian Cobra lives. It is found across North Africa today, as far south as Zambia. It is rather larger than the more familiar Indian Cobra (*Naja naja*), but doesn't spread its hood so widely and is not marked with the familiar black spectacles.

ASS

There are 84 references to the domesticated ass; the WILD ASS is treated separately (q.v.). Few animals are more frequently mentioned in the Bible and the ass played a central part in life, not only for riding, but also as a beast of burden and, more rarely, for ploughing. Moses rode an ass when he and his wife and two sons passed through the desert of Sinai (Ex 4:20) and Balaam was riding his she-ass when it saw the angel of the Lord before he did (Num 22:21-33); Achsah rode an ass (Jos 15:18) as did the 30 sons of Jair (Jud 10:3) and the sons of Abdon (Jud 12:14), Abigail (1 Sam 25:20), Ahithophel (2 Sam 17:23) and Mephibosheth (2 Sam 19:26), as did the unnamed prophet who was slain because he dined in defiance of the word of the Lord (1 Kings 13).

The best-known journey on an ass is that of Christ on his entry into Jerusalem, in fulfilment of the prophecy (Zech 9:9), which has been much illustrated and discussed, and as much misunderstood because it is often quoted as an example of meekness and lowliness of heart, a public gesture of humility. But the ass was a perfectly respectable mount, as illustrated, and was in common use. The point of the story in Matthew 21:7 is not that Christ was humbling himself, but that he came as a man of peace. The horse was the animal of war, the mount of the conqueror (see HORSE). Asses were ridden by persons of rank, but not by military leaders in time of war. So Christ came, not as conqueror, but as the bearer of the message of peace.

As a beast of burden, the ass first makes an appearance when Abraham took his son and the load of wood to the land of Moriah to make his sacrifice, where the context clearly suggests that the wood was loaded on the ass (Gen 22:3); and the sons of Jacob certainly loaded their asses with corn (Gen 42:26, 27); the gifts which Joseph sent to his father from Egypt were loaded on 20 asses (Gen 45:23); and Jesse sent David to Saul with an ass-load of goods (1 Sam 16:20). When Abigail sought to soften the vengeance of David, she loaded a remarkable 200 loaves of bread, 2 skins of wine, 5 sheep, 17 kilogrammes of roasted grain, 100 bunches of raisins and 200 cakes of dried figs onto asses and rode over to him; the provisions for David's coronation at Hebron were loaded onto asses (1 Chron 12:40), and asses were used to carry the

Somali Wild Ass (*Equus asinus*)

'The ox knoweth his owner and the ass his master's crib.' (Isaiah 1:3)

produce of the harvest (Neh 13:15). The ass was, and still is, the most common beast of burden in Bible lands.

That asses were used in ploughing is implied in the prohibition of Deuteronomy 22:10, which forbids them to be yoked together with oxen; a very practical measure, since the rhythm of work and the pace of stepping of the two are so dissimilar that to yoke them together would be to cause hardship to both. This has also been interpreted as an instance of the Mosaic law's general prohibition on intermixtures: priests were not allowed patched garments, piebald cattle could not be offered in sacrifice, a garment might not be made of linen and wool, and different domestic animals were not allowed to breed (see MULE).

Ass's milk was drunk but the flesh of the ass was forbidden by Mosaic law because it has an undivided hoof and chews the cud. It is an indication of the severity of the famine at the siege of Samaria that we are told an ass's head was sold for 80 pieces of silver (2 Kings 6:25).

In Jewish legend the ass, in common with the rest of the animal kingdom, is used to point a moral: it was observed to have the habit of smelling its excrement and then urinating. The legend is that the donkey complained to God that it should not have to work for man without compensation and threatened to refrain from propagating its species unless God allowed a fair wage for its work. God told the donkey that its wish would be fulfilled when its urine flowed in a stream that would work a water-mill and its excrement smelled like flowers. So donkeys are constantly checking to see if they yet measure up.

BADGER

The animal is mentioned 14 times, but always with reference to its skin, which is used as an offering: 'And this is the offering which ye shall take of them … rams' skins dyed red and badgers' skins and shittim wood' (Exod 25:5), and as covering for the feet: 'I clothed thee also with broidered work, and shod thee with badgers' skin, and girded thee about with fine linen' (Ezek 16:10), and above all as a covering for the Ark of the Covenant: 'And thou shalt make a covering for the tent of

Honey Badger (*Mellivora capensis*)

'I clothed thee also with broidered work, and shod thee with badger's skin.' (Ezekiel 16:10)

rams' skins dyed red and a covering of badgers' skins' (Exod 26:14. See also Exod 35:7, 35:23, 36:19, 39:34; Num 4:6, 8, 10, 11, 14 and 25).

The point is that live Badgers are nowhere mentioned in the Bible, although *Meles meles* and *Mellivora capensis* have been recorded in Bible lands. Their skin is tough and durable, but unlikely to have been available in the desert in Sufficient numbers to have provided a covering for the Ark, although Badger skins were on sale in leather shops in Canon Tristram's time. So there is dispute about this translation.

An attractive alternative is 'porpoise', since the Arabic for this is *Tuchash*, which is close to the Hebrew *Tahash*, the word in question. There is some evidence that seal skins were used as coverings in ancient times, and Pliny reports that they were particularly suitable for the coverings of the roofs of buildings, since it was believed that lightning never struck this material. This is the alternative chosen by NAS. Of the other modern versions, GNB and JB have 'fine leather'; NIV has 'hides of sea cows'; AB has 'dolphin, or porpoise skins'; NEB has 'Porpoise hides', with a footnote which adds 'strictly, sea cow'; and RAV stays with 'badger skins'. There is a Hebrew legend that the *Tahash* was a creature specially created by God so that its skin could be used for the outer covering of the Tabernacle. Once the Tabernacle had been built, the *Tahash*, having fulfilled its function, disappeared. It had a single horn on its forehead, was gaily coloured like a turkey cock, and was classified as a clean animal, so enormous that a curtain 30 cubits long could be made from one skin.

The Badger, being a nocturnal animal and very shy of humans, had the reputation in AV times of having magical powers. In *Hortus Sanitatis*, published in the late fifteenth and early sixteenth centuries, is a full account of its shape and qualities:

The Brock has short legs, and not equal on the two sides, but shorter on the left side, so that planting the feet of the right side in the ruts made by wheels, it runs valiantly and escapes its pursuers. The fat of the badger grows when the moon waxes, and decreases as it wanes, so that, if it be killed on the last day of the old moon none is found. This is strange, that, though this part of the beast is medicinal, yet its bite is very often serious and fatal; and the reason of this is that it lives on wasps, and animals which creep on the ground and are venomous, and therefore they infect its teeth. Its brain boiled with oil cures all pains.

B AT

Lesser Short-tailed Bat (*Rhinopomia hardwickei*)

'In that day a man shall cast his idols . . . to the moles and to the bats.' (Isaiah 2:20)

There are two occasions for the mention of this creature: one in the list of unclean birds, where it is grouped with the Lapwing and the stork (Lev 11:19 and Deut 14:18); and in the description of the desolation of the last days given by Isaiah: 'In that day a man shall cast his idols of silver and his idols of gold, which they made, each one for himself to worship, to the moles and to the bats' (Isaiah 2:20).

The Hebrew word is *Atalef* and there is agreement that it refers to the order *Chiroptera* which, of course, are not birds, although they are normally seen flying through the dusk or dawn skies, where they are as expert in that element as the most skilled of winged creatures and so the classification in Leviticus is not inappropriate. It is also clear that they would be thought of as unclean, since bats are among the most malodorous of flying creatures, although the large fruit bats are eaten today in parts of Africa, the skin being first carefully removed so as not to transfer its smell to the flesh.

Because bats frequent ruins and caves, because they sleep upside down during the day and emerge to hunt at night, and because they swoop swiftly and silently avoiding obstacles at great speed in almost total darkness, they have often been credited with demonic powers and were associated with witches in the time of the AV translation. Albertus Magnus had written, in his book *Of the Wonders of the World*: 'If you wish to see anything submerged and deep in the night, and that it may not be more hidden from thee than in the day, and that you may read books in the dark night, — anoint your face with the blood of a bat and that will happen which I say.'

In Bible lands there are over 20 species of bat, most of them small and insectivorous, including the Short-tailed Bat (*Pipistrellus kuhli*), which Canon Tristram found in quarries under the Temple of Jerusalem and in the Cave of Adullam, swarming so thickly that it was difficult to keep a torch alight when crawling through the caverns.

 BEAR

This animal is mentioned 13 times in the Old Testament and once in the New. It is famed for its savagery and attacks both flocks and their keepers, as in the account which David gives to Saul of the assaults made by both Lion and bear on his flock (1 Sam 17:34) and also the she-bear which acted as an agent of destruction of the Lord in killing the 42 children who mocked at Elisha's bald head (2 Kings 2:24). The most dangerous animal of all to encounter was the she-bear robbed of her cubs which is mentioned in 2 Sam 17:3, Prov 17:12, and Hos 13:8, possibly from the experience which many hunters had when trying to obtain cubs to rear and train for the circuses of the day. The wicked ruler is compared to 'a roaring lion or a ranging bear' (Prov 28:15); and one of the signs of the peaceable kingdom is that the cow will feed side by side with the bear, its natural enemy (Isaiah 11:7). The roaring, or moaning, of the bear is in Isaiah 59:11, and its stealthiness, its 'lying in wait in secret places' in Lam 3:10. Its extreme destructiveness is in Dan 7:5, where the second, Median kingdom is likened to a bear which is told to 'arise, devour much flesh'; and, in Amos, the book of a shepherd, we have the proverbial expression 'as if a man did flee from a lion and a bear met him' (Amos 5:19). The New Testament reference is to the Beast of the Book of Revelations, which is described as 'like unto a leopard, his feet were as the feet of a bear, and his mouth was as the mouth of a lion' (Rev 13:2).

There is a strange story in Hebrew lore which tells of the bear being created without breasts, so God made the young of the bear suck their paws until they were old enough to care for themselves. And the AV translators would have been familiar with the legend which has led to our phrase, 'to lick into shape'. As recorded by the naturalist Bartholomew: 'The whelp is a piece of flesh little more than a mouse having neither eyes nor hair and having claws somedeal burgeoning and so this lump she licketh and so shapeth a whelp with licking.'

The Brown Bear (*Ursus arctos*) is found over a large part of the northern hemisphere and is an interesting example of Bergmann's law, which says that in any given species the most northerly representatives are the biggest. So the Mediterranean Brown Bear normally grows to around 450 pounds in weight, whereas its relative in North America can reach 1,550 pounds. Although the Elizabethan notions of the cubs being born as an unformed mass which is then licked into shape by the mother have gone unsupported by field observation, it has been established that the cubs, normally two, are at birth little bigger than rats and are quite helpless and cling close to their mother until the autumn, when the time comes to put down fat for the hibernation. Brown Bears live mainly on fruit, honey, insects, and just occasionally on grass and dead animals.

Syrian Bear (*Ursus arctos syriacus*)

'Let a bear robbed of her whelps meet a man, rather than a fool in his folly.' (Proverbs 17:12)

BEE

Bees
(Photograph:
Treat Davidson)

'They compassed me
about like bees; they are
quenched as the fire of
thorns.' (Psalm 118:12)

Three of the four references to bees clearly refer to the wild
stocks that swarm in the many fissures of rocks that flank the
valleys in Bible lands. They are so savage that, if disturbed, they
are able to attack and chase away any who would plunder their
honeycombs, so the ferocity of the most formidable of the
Canaanite nations is compared to them: 'And the Amorites ...
came out against you and chased you as bees do' (Deut 1:44).
And the psalmist, pressed on all sides by the nations of the
unbelievers, cries out 'They compassed me about like bees'
(Psa 118:12). Isaiah prophesies that, at the time of the sign
from the Lord when a virgin shall conceive and bear a son, 'the
Lord shall hiss for the fly that is in the uttermost part of the
rivers of Egypt, and for the bee that is in the land of Assyria' as
a force of destruction upon the land (Isaiah 7:18).

Our own image of the bee as the gentle, blossom-kissing harbinger of summer was not shared by the people of Old Testament times; there is a Jewish legend which tells of the daughter of a rich man of the city of Admah who gave bread and water to a stranger in defiance of the law and was taken by the people, smothered with honey and left to be stung to death by bees as a penalty. Even the AV translators, living in the age when Ariel first sang 'Where the bee sucks there suck I', had a sterner view of the habits of bees from the naturalist Bartholomew:

> They have an host and a king and move war and battle, and fly and void smoke and wind, and make them hardy and sharp to battle with great noise ... And no creature is more wreakful nor more fervent to take wreak than is the bee when he is wroth; therefore a multitude of a great host of bees throweth down great hedges when they be compelled to withstand them that destroy their honey.

However, the fourth reference to bees, which is the best known, calls up their place in the land as the providers of sweetness. After Samson has killed the young lion with his bare hands he returns to the carcase and 'behold there was a swarm of bees and honey in the carcase of the lion' (Judges 14:8). And out of the strong came forth sweetness. The most frequently quoted description of Canaan is that it was to be a land 'flowing with milk and honey' (Exod 3:8), and there are many contexts in the Bible in which honey is associated with that which is wholesome and good: the words of the Lord are 'sweeter than honey' (Psa 19:10). There is an interesting apparent contradiction in Proverbs, which tells us, 'My son, eat thou honey because it is good' (Prov 24:13), and in the very next chapter warns 'It is not good to eat much honey: so for men to search their own glory is not glory' (Prov 25:27). Of course we are being told that you can have too much of even a good thing.

The Hebrew word here is *Dvora*, which, in its form *Deborah*, not only refers to the Honey Bee (*Apis mellifera*), but was also a name popular in the age of the Patriarchs (Gen 35:8). The insect is probably the most deeply studied in the world and has been associated with man since the earliest times: Virgil, Aristotle, Cicero and Pliny all eulogised the bee as the richest of insects in the benefits it confers on mankind and there is a hieroglyphic bee on the sarcophagus of Mykerinos which dates back to around 3600 BC.

BEETLE

There is only one reference and this is to the admissibility of this creature as an article of food: 'Yet these ye may eat of every flying creeping thing that goes upon all four, which have legs above their feet to leap withal upon the earth ... the locust after his kind and the beetle after his kind' (Lev 11:21-2).

The Hebrew word is *Hargol* and there is some dispute as to the translation because beetles, properly so called, which belong to the order *Coleoptera*, do not have legs above their feet to leap withal upon the earth, as do the locusts, nor are they ever, as are the locusts, an item of diet.

So, although the beetles are the largest of the orders of insects, with more than 250,000 species ranging from the Hercules and Goliath beetles of tropical lands which can weigh up to 100 grams to the smallest range of insects less than 0.5mm long, many of which are found in Bible lands, modern translators have all abandoned the word 'beetle' here and have substituted either 'GRASSHOPPER' or 'LOCUST' (q.v.).

Scarab beetle (*Scarabaeus sacer*)

'Every one of them ye may eat ... the beetle after his kind.' (Leviticus 11:22)

BEHEMOTH

Because there has been a great deal of dispute among scholars about this creature, it is worth while considering the whole of the only passage in which it occurs:

15 Behold now behemoth, which I made with thee; he eateth grass as an ox.
16 Lo, now, his strength is in his loins, and his force is in the navel of his belly.
17 He moveth his tail like a cedar: the sinews of his stones are wrapped together.
18 His bones are as strong pieces of brass; his bones are like bars of iron.
19 He is the chief of the ways of God: he that made him can make his sword to approach unto him.
20 Surely the mountains bring him forth food where all the beasts of the field play.
21 He lieth under the shady trees, in the covert of the reed and fens.
22 The shade trees cover him with their shadow; the willows of the brook compass him about.
23 Behold he drinketh up a river and hasteth not: he trusteth that he can draw up Jordan into his mouth.
24 He taketh it with his eyes: his nose pierceth through snares.

(Job 40:15-24)

Now the interpreters of this passage can be divided into the mythological and the zoological, the first pointing out that a mythical beast called the Behemoth is known in Hebrew legend and the second that the setting of this passage is so naturalistic that the creature can be identified. They then divide on the identification. The word 'Behemoth' is an intensification of the word *behemah*, meaning a beast, and it is frequently used and translated elsewhere as 'great beasts' or simply for cattle, herds, or wild beasts where the context clearly indicates that this is appropriate. But the opening verse here, especially the words 'which I made with thee', does seem to point to the mythical beast the Behemoth which, according to Hebrew legend, was formed by God on the sixth day of Creation, like the rest of the mammals, out of solid earth. And, just as

Leviathan is the greatest of the fishes, so Behemoth is the greatest creature on land. He matches Leviathan in size and strength; so God, having created Behemoth male and female, deprived him of the desire to propagate to prevent his race from dominating the earth. There is a reference to verse 20 in the legend that Behemoth needed the produce of a thousand mountains a day to keep him in food, and to verse 23 in the legend that all the water flowing through Jordan for a year was only sufficient for one of his gulps. He had to be granted, entirely for his own use, a stream that flowed from Paradise, called Yubal. Behemoth, like Leviathan, was destined to be a reward for the pious in afterlife: having denied themselves the pleasures of watching gladiatorial combats in the circuses, they would be allowed to see a fight to the death between Leviathan and Behemoth and would then be served the flesh of both monsters at a banquet.

The zoological interpreters have pointed out, however, that much of the description here is naturalistic, especially the setting, with shady trees and the willows of the brook. They have been divided into the proponents of the elephant, the crocodile and the Hippopotamus as creatures to which the text was referring. In modern times, the Hippopotamus has won the

Hippopotamus
(*Hippopotamus amphibius*)

'Behold now behemoth, which I made with thee: he eateth grass as an ox.' (Job 40:15)

day, though the NEB stands alone in preferring crocodile. In their support, the hippopotamists claim that the Hebrew word *behemoth* is connected with the Egyptian word for Hippopotamus *p-ehe-mou*, (water ox); that the animal is herbivorous (v. 15); that it is stout of body (v. 16); that its tail is thick and rigid and its legs sinewy (v. 17); its bones are solid (v. 18); that it dwells in swamps (v. 21); and is familiar with the inundation of the Nile (v. 23). Finally, and most persuasively, they point out that the Hippopotamus is the largest animal indigenous to Bible lands.

It seems most likely that we have a mixture of ideas here, some drawn from mythology and some from the observation of nature. The swamp-dwelling, grass-eating creature which is hunted by hooks could well be the Hippopotamus – there are Egyptian wall paintings which record this method of hunting; but the size and strength and diet of the creature have strong overtones of myth. God is here contrasting the puny and insignificant physical attributes of man with the greatest of His creations and the moral is pointed the more forcibly where myth and nature combine.

BITTERN

One of the most sonorously evocative of the creatures in this book, the Bittern has sadly been lost from modern translations. It is used to convey the impression of a lonely and desolate region: 'I will make it a possession for the bittern and pools of water: and I will sweep it with the besom of destruction' (Isaiah 14:23); so the prophet speaks against Babylon. And against Idumaea he pronounces 'the cormorant and the bittern shall possess it; the owl also and the raven shall dwell in it' (Isaiah 34:11). And Zephaniah cries out 'He will make Nineveh a desolation ... both the cormorant and the bittern shall lodge in the upper lintels of it; their voice shall sing in the windows; desolation shall be in the threshold' (Zep 2:13-14).

The Bittern is certainly a powerful ally for the prophet of desolation, and none of the alternative translations suggested for the Hebrew *Kippod*: 'porcupine', 'hedgehog', 'tortoise', and 'bustard', or even the favourite among modern translations:

'owl', can quite convey the mood as does this solitary bird, with its superb camouflage and its haunting, booming call so impossible to locate when heard across lonely marshlands at dusk.

The Bittern (*Botaurus stellaris*), although quite a large bird and little smaller than a heron, is very rarely seen as it inhabits reed beds and the tall vegetation around lakesides. If disturbed, it stretches its long thin neck vertically into the air like the slim stem of a sapling and merges with its background. It is a solitary nester and remains hidden during the day, but occasionally may be glimpsed at dusk flying low over the reed tops with slowly beating wings and hunched shoulders. It feeds on eels for choice, but will also eat worms, frogs, voles and even the young of other birds.

Bittern (*Botaurus stellaris*)

'I will make it a possession for the bittern and pools of water.' (Isaiah 14:23)

BOAR

Wild Boar (*Sus scrofa*)

'The boar out of the wood doth waste it, and the wild beast of the field doth devour it.' (Psalm 80:13)

Although there is only one mention of the boar, the Hebrew word *Chazir* also means 'swine' and is separately treated (see SWINE). The Wild Boar is the one mentioned by the psalmist, which lays waste the vineyard: 'The boar out of the wood doth waste it, and the wild beast of the field doth devour it' (Psa 80:13). The Wild Boar (*Sus scrofa*) was very plentiful in Bible lands only a century ago. Canon Tristram found them swarming in the thickets all along the banks of the Jordan from Jericho to the Lake of Gennesaret and, although they are the most unclean of animals to both Jew and Moslem, he was able to taste of the flesh which he described as 'bearing the same relation to pork as venison does to mutton'. It had another special virtue: so long as the larder contained the flesh of the Wild Boar, it was safe from pilfering, since none of the guides would risk pollution from coming into contact with it. The ancestor of the domestic pig was a forest dweller, living on anything it could find from the roots of trees and fruit to the eggs and young of birds and even small mammals. Wild Boar were so plentiful in ancient times that a legend of the Jews told how God, every seven years, transformed Nature and the Wild Boar sprang from the mountain mouse.

Some commentators have identified the 'wild boar from the wood' with the Roman legions, since the Roman legion stationed in Palestine had, as its standard, the emblem of a wild boar.

CAMEL

There are no identification problems here. In fact, the Hebrew word *Gamal* is the origin of our own. It is one of the earliest animals to be mentioned in the Bible: Abraham had large numbers of Camels (Gen 24:10) and also Jacob (Gen 30:43, 31:34); and they were carriers between Arabia and Egypt (Gen 37:25). The Ethiopians had Camels in abundance (2 Chron 14:15) and also, of course, the Queen of Sheba (1 Kings 10:2); the Midianites and Amelakites had them 'as the sand by the seaside for multitude' (Judges 7:12). Camels were used for riding in peace (Gen 24:61), the Midianites and Amelakites

One-humped Camel
(*Camelus dromedarius*)

'And their camels shall
be a booty...'
(Jeremiah 49:32)

rode them in war (1 Sam 30:17) and they were used to draw chariots (Isaiah 21:7). They were part of the self-presentation to the world of the rich: their trappings were sometimes trimmed with gold (Judges 8:21).

The Hebrews were forbidden to eat Camel flesh (Lev 11:4), though there is a Hebrew legend that the fallen angels consumed a thousand a day and, although the drinking of camel milk is not expressly mentioned, there is reference to the gift which Jacob gave to Esau of 'thirty milch camels with their colts' (Gen 32:15). The skins of Camels were used for sandals.

Of the three contexts in which Camel occurs in the New Testament, one is realistic, to the Camel's hair clothing worn by John the Baptist (Mark 1:6), and the other two are proverbial: the use, by Jesus, of the largest animal familiar to his hearers to point a moral. Firstly, when he rebukes the hypocrisy of the scribes and the Pharisees, calling them 'blind guides which strain at a gnat and swallow a camel' (Matt 23:24), and secondly when he cautions the rich with the words 'it is easier for a camel to go through the eye of a needle than for a rich man to enter the kingdom of God' (Matt 19:24).

At the time of the AV translation, the Camel was a rarely heard of exotic beast which had been mentioned five times in Shakespeare's plays, and had the reputation of being disdainful and malcontent. Strangely, it shared with man two of life's burdens: baldness and gout. The naturalist Bartholomew records: 'Among four-footed beasts, camels wax bald as men do, as well as the ostrich and certain beasts among fowls. Camels have the podagra [gout] and the frenzy, and by the podagra their feet be strained, and this evil slayeth them sometimes.'

Camels have existed in Bible lands for over a million years, as testified by the bones identified in Pleistocene deposits. Superbly adapted to desert conditions, the Camel has nostrils that will close against the fine sand, deep eye sockets protected by long lashes, mouth parts that seem totally insensitive to the thorns and dry bushes it eats, and broad cushioned feet that do not sink into the sand as well as the more obvious hump of spongy tissue that enables it to travel for a week without water.

CANKERWORM

An insect which is mentioned by the prophets Joel and Nahum as an agent of destruction: 'I will restore to you the years that the locust hath eaten, the cankerworm and the caterpillar' (Joel 2:25); and this is to happen only if the people are repentant and can avoid the plague in which 'that which the cankerworm hath left hath the caterpillar eaten' (Joel 1:4). The prophet Nahum, foretelling the doom of the city of Nineveh, capital of Assyria, cries that the fire 'shall eat thee up like the cankerworm: make thyself many as the cankerworm, make thy self many as the locusts. Thou hast multiplied thy merchants above the stars of heaven: the cankerworm spoileth and flyeth away' (Nahum 3:15-16).

The Hebrew word is *Jelek* and modern translators are satisfied that it refers to a stage in the development of the Locust, probably at the nymph form. The word 'canker', from a root meaning gangrene, was used of a spreading sore or ulcer and so of anything which corrupts or consumes slowly and secretly. The canker in the heart of the rose was the common figure for the inevitable decay which lies in all beauty. A powerful image which enriches the text here but which has been abandoned by modern translators.

Migratory Locusts
(*Locusta migratoria*)
(Photograph:
Frank Lane)

'It shall eat thee up, like the cankerworm'
Nahum 3:15)

CATERPILLAR

Like the previous entry, this word has now been largely accepted as referring to a stage in the development of the LOCUST (q.v.). There are two Hebrew words so translated, *Jelek* and *Hasil,* and they both occur in contexts which imply a threat or a plague: 'If there be in the land famine, if there be pestilence ... or if there be caterpillar' (1 Kings 8:37 and 2 Chron 6:28); 'He gave also their increase unto the caterpillar and their labour unto the locust' (Psa 78:46). The parallelism in Isaiah strongly suggests an identification with the Locust: 'And your spoil shall be gathered like the gathering of the caterpillar: as the running to and fro of locusts shall he run upon them' (Isaiah 33:4). The psalmist, celebrating the works of the Lord in the form of the plagues which He sent on Egypt, sings 'He spake and the locusts came and caterpillars and that without number' (Psa 105:34). And Jeremiah celebrates the Lord's judgement on Babylon in defence of Israel: 'He spake, and locusts came, and caterpillars, and that without number' (Jer

51:14) and 'blow the trumpet among the nations ... cause the horses to come up as the rough caterpillars' (Jer 51:27).

It is very difficult for us, with the possible exception of keen gardeners, to think of the caterpillar as a threat. We are nurtured with the notions of the woolly caterpillar of Little Arabella Miller and the amiable and bumbling creature in *Alice in Wonderland*. But, to the translators of AV times, the caterpillar had been recorded by naturalists as a menace. Topsell's *History of Serpents* says: 'There is not any one sort of Caterpillars but they are malign, naught, and venomous ... Caterpillars mixed with oil do drive away serpents.'

CATTLE

There are six different names for cattle in the Bible and they are mentioned 450 times. Because they were the most important possessions of a nomadic people they tend to be equated with the term used for possessions in general, as is still remembered in the legal term 'chattels', derived from the same word and meaning movable, tangible articles of property.

Cattle were used in agricultural work on the threshing floor: 'Thou shalt not muzzle the ox when he treadeth out the corn' (Deut 24:5); as pack animals: 'They brought bread ... on mules and on oxen' (1 Chron 12:40); they were hitched to wagons: 'they brought their offerings before the Lord, six covered wagons and twelve oxen' (Num 7:3); and the Ark of the Lord was drawn by 'two milch kine on which there has come no yoke' (1 Sam 6:7). Cattle were so essential to everyday living in Bible lands that the Mosaic laws made special provisions for them: they were to be included in the Sabbath day of rest, 'on the seventh day shalt thou rest that thine ox and thine ass may rest' (Exod 23:12); and the familial duty enjoined on a brother extended to his cattle, 'Thou shalt not see thy brother's ox or his sheep go astray' (Deut 22:1). Indeed the care of cattle was so essential that it was to go beyond the bounds of kinship or friendship: 'If thou meet thine enemy's ox or his ass going astray, thou shalt surely bring it back to him again' (Exod 23:4).

Cattle with Cattle Egret (*Bubulcus ibis*)

'If thou meet thine enemies ox . . . going astray, thou shalt surely bring it back to him again.' (Exodus 23:4)

A fallen ox had to be helped to its feet (Deut 22:4) and an ox should not be yoked to a plough with an ass (Deut 22:10); an ox which gored a man or woman to death was stoned to death itself, but then might not be eaten (Exod 21:28). An ox which merely pushed a servant was stoned and the master fined (Exod 21:32). There is an interesting foretaste of our own legal code in which a pet dog is allowed one bite: if an ox is known to have 'pushed' before and the matter has been testified to the owner, then, should it gore someone to death, both it and its master were put to death (Exod 21:29).

Cattle, being the most prized of possessions, were considered the most valuable of sacrifices: Solomon was the most splendid in this, offering 22,000 as a peace offering (1 Kings 8:63) and, on another occasion, he sacrificed before the ark 'sheep and oxen which could not be told nor numbered for multitude' (2 Chron 5:6). The cattle of Bible times were, of course, much closer to wild cattle than the sleek products of selective breeding of our own day. They would tend to be horned and shaggy, rather like smaller versions of highland cattle, left to roam for much of the year on the lean pastures. Or in the winter, to be fattened for the table, brought in and fed barley straw in their stalls; a practice which gave rise to one of the most telling images in the Bible: 'Better is a dinner of herbs where love is, than a stalled ox and hatred therewith' (Prov 15:17).

CHAMELEON

Found only once, in the list of unclean animals in Leviticus 11:30. There are problems with the identification of the animals listed in this verse, since no context is given which allows a clear classification to be made, but the chameleon, unlike the other animals in this verse, has survived in most of the modern translations.

The Hebrew word is *Koach*, which means, basically, strength. This has led some commentators to suggest that the Monitor lizard (*Varanus griseus*), the largest and most powerful of its class, is meant but the Chameleon (*Chamaeleo chamaeleon*) has quite enough bizarre physical characteristics to ensure it a place on any list of creatures to be avoided.

Its eyes are set high on its head in sockets that can move independently; it can change its appearance with a wide variety of different colorations; and it can suddenly shoot out a tongue that extends beyond the length of its head and body together. Desert dwellers would need little encouragement to avoid this most unnerving of lizards.

The AV translators, having available to them Topsell's *History of Serpents*, would have felt secure in including the chameleon among the creatures to be wary of:

> If the Chameleon at any time see a serpent taking the air, and sunning himself under some green tree, and settleth himself directly over the serpent, then out of his mouth he casteth a thread like a spider, at the end whereof hangeth a drop of poison as bright as any pearl, which lighting upon the serpent killeth it immediately. The right claw of the forefeet, bound to the left arm with the skin of his cheeks, is good against robberies and terrors of the night, and the right pap against all fears. If the left foot be scorched in a furnace with the herb Chameleon, and afterward putting a little ointment to it and made into little pasties, so being carried about in a wooden box, it maketh the party to go invisible. Likewise the liver dissolveth amorous enchantments. The entrails and dung of this beast, washed in the urine of an ape, and hung up at our enemy's gates, causeth reconciliation.

There are about 80 species of chameleon, mostly found in

Chameleon
(*Chamaeleo chamaeleon*)

'These also shall be unclean unto you among the creeping things that creep upon the earth ... the ferret and the chameleon and the lizard.' (Leviticus 11:30)

Africa south of the Sahara, but the Common Chameleon occurs along the shores of the Mediterranean. Although it used to be thought that the colour changes of the chameleon were a form of camouflage, enabling it to adapt to whatever surroundings it happened to be in, latest researches suggest that these alterations in pigmentation are simply responses to changes in light intensity, temperature, or even emotional state. Chameleons are thus able to tell how other chameleons are feeling by their colour. Some can go black with rage.

Because chameleons often live in harsh conditions where there is little evidence of food it used to be thought they could live on air. Hamlet, when asked about his health, replies 'Excellent i'faith. Of the chameleon's dish. I eat the air, promise-crammed.'

CHAMOIS

Together with the wild ox, the Chamois is one of the animals which is listed as permitted food (Deut 14:15) and this is its only mention. The Hebrew word is *Zemer* and it occurs as Chamois only in the AV. The RSV amended the translation to 'mountain sheep'. There is a cognate word in Arabic, *zamar*, which refers to a leaping animal and the modern translators mostly prefer to stay with the RSV and have here 'mountain sheep'. The Chamois (*Rupicapra rupicapra*) is found in the Pyrenees and the Alps and has not been recorded wild in Bible lands.

Cyprus Sheep (*Ovis ammon ophion*)

'These are the beasts which ye shall eat . . . the wild ox and the chamois.' (Deuteronomy 14:5)

CHICKEN

Only mentioned once, in one of the most moving passages of the New Testament, where Jesus cries out over Jerusalem: 'Oh Jerusalem, Jerusalem . . . how often would I have gathered thy children together, even as a hen gathereth her chickens under her wings.' See entry under HEN.

COCK

Cockerel (*Gallus domesticus*)

'Before the cock crow thou shalt deny me.' (Luke 22:61)

There is mention of the cock crowing, which the AV gives as one word, in the passage in Mark, where Jesus warns that the Son of Man is as a man taking a far journey who tells the servants of his house to watch for his return: 'Watch ye therefore, for ye know not when the master of the house cometh, at even, or at midnight, or at the cockcrowing, or in the morning.' It is interesting that the cock crowing here is set between midnight and the morning, whereas we tend to associate the crowing of the cock with dawn. But in the country it soon comes to our notice that the first sounds of crowing that we hear are in the hours of darkness, and there is a long-established tradition, dating back to AV times, that the cock is, as Horatio put it, 'the trumpet to the morn' and crows while it is yet dark to warn the midnight spirits that roam the earth to return to the lower regions before the first streaks of day.

The only other situation in which the crowing of the cock features is that of the betrayal by Peter, recorded in all four gospels (Matt 26:34, 74; Mark 14:30, 68, 72; Luke 22:34, 60, 61; John 13:38, 18:27). Mark alone mentions that the cock crowed twice, and there was a convention that, at pascal time, the first cock crow would be around 2.30 a.m. and the second at 5 a.m.

There is a Hebrew legend that the cock is the greatest of the singers of praise of the Almighty: when God, at midnight, goes to the pious in paradise, all the trees break out in adoration and their songs awaken the cock who, in turn, praises God with seven hymns. The crowing of the cock is seen today as the heralding of the light which drives away the demons and a reminder to man that he has a duty daily to praise God.

COCKATRICE

There are four mentions of this fabulous creature in the Old Testament, three of which are in the prophet Isaiah, who warns that 'out of the serpent's root shall come forth a cockatrice, and his fruit shall be a fiery flying serpent' (Isaiah 14:29). He tells of the poisonous nature of the beast: 'They hatch cockatrice's eggs ... he that eateth of their eggs dieth' (Isaiah 59:5). And in the peaceable kingdom the 'weaned child shall put his hand on the cockatrice's den' (Isaiah 11:8). The prophet Jeremiah has the fourth reference: 'Behold, I will send serpents, cockatrice among you which will not be charmed, and they shall bite you, saith the Lord' (Jer 8:17).

The Hebrew words are *Tsepha* and *Tsiphoni*, which all modern translations have rendered as 'VIPER' or 'ADDER' (q.v.), with the sole exception of the JB which keeps 'basilisk' for the reference in Isaiah 14:29.

So natural history has triumphed over myth in our time. The AV translators were better acquainted with the nature of the beast they were referring to, and it was quite adequate to inspire the terrors intended, being the product of a cock's egg hatched by a serpent. It could set fire to bushes and break up rocks to powder just by breathing on them; its venom was so potent that Pliny reports a mounted man who, stabbing one with a long spear, was killed by the poison that travelled up the haft of the spear. The cockatrice was said to be fearless, except that it had a secret terror of the cock, and so travellers who had to pass through the lands where cockatrices were known to live would carry cocks with them as a form of protection. The cockatrice was fond of eating weasels and yet could be killed by the weasel's bite; the cockatrice could also kill the weasel with its poison unless the weasel, having been bitten, could quickly eat of the herb rue.

Cockatrice

'I will send serpents, cockatrices among you, which will not be charmed.' (Jeremaiah 8:17)

CONEY

This animal is first mentioned as unclean 'because he cheweth the cud but divideth not the hoof' (Lev 11:5 and Deut 14:7). It lives in the wilderness: 'The high hills are a refuge for the wild goats and the rocks for the conies' (Psa 104:18). And they are mentioned in Proverbs as among the four things which are

little upon the earth and yet are exceeding wise: 'The conies are but a feeble folk, yet they make their houses among the rocks' (Prov 30:26). At the time of the AV translation, the word 'cony' meant, simply, 'rabbit', from the Latin *cuniculus*. It was translated from the Hebrew *Shafan*, which means 'hider', and so could refer to a number of the small mammals that hide among the rocks in Bible lands.

Modern translators are agreed that the animal referred to is the Rock Hyrax, or Syrian Hyrax (*Procavia capensis syriaca*), an animal that has nothing to do with rabbits or rodents generally, but is a distant relative to the rhinoceros and the elephant, having molar teeth that are tiny versions of those of the rhinoceros, and broad nails. They have rounded ears and are often seen sunning themselves in the open on the rocky slopes of the valleys. They do not chew the cud but the Hebrew word here can also be understood as meaning re-chew, and these small mammals certainly have the characteristic that their jaws are always on the move. They are well characterised as wise, though feeble, in that they make their nest among the crevices of the rocks and usually feed in groups nearby with a sentry posted whose first squeak of alarm sends them, in the wink of an eye, back to their holes.

Rock Hyrax (*Procavia capensis syriaca*)

'The conies are but a feeble folk, yet they make their houses among the rocks.' (Proverbs 30:26)

Cormorant

Cormorant
(*Phalacrocorax carbo*)

'None shall pass through it for ever and ever. But the cormorant and the bittern shall possess it . . .'
(Isaiah 34:10-11)

Among the birds which are to be held in abomination by the Israelites are 'the little owl, the cormorant, and the great owl' (Lev 11:13-17) and the Hebrew word here is *Shalak*, which modern translators have retained as cormorant. There are, however, two other references in which the cormorant is the symbol of desolation: 'none shall pass through it for ever and ever. But the cormorant and the bittern shall possess it' (Isaiah 34:10-11); and 'he ... will make Nineveh a desolation ... both the cormorant and the bittern shall lodge in the upper lintels of it' (Zeph 2:13-14). And here another word is used, the Hebrew *Qath*, which modern translators have rendered with a species of owl since owls are more likely to be found inhabiting ruins and the cormorant is unlikely to be settled far from water. Some authorities have translated *Qath* as pelican, but this seems even less likely than the cormorant to be found lodging in a lintel.

We lose many sinister overtones by preferring owls here: Milton uses the cormorant as the symbol of Satan, hunched in a tree and plotting the downfall of Adam and Eve; Mantegna's famous painting, *The Agony in the Garden*, has the dark shape of the cormorant perched high over the garden of Gethsemane and bleakly staring at the praying Christ. The very name is redolent of blackness and the wastes of the sea: *Corvus marinus*, the sea raven.

There are two species of cormorant commonly found around the Mediterranean, *Phalacrocorax carbo* and *Phalacrocorax desmarestii*. Canon Tristram also came across the Pygmy Cormorant (*Phalacrocorax pygmeus*) on the Kishon and the Litany. The bird certainly looks sinister: it is the largest all-dark European sea bird and has a long beak, hooked at the end, with white patches at its base and also on each thigh. It nests in the open on patches of bare rock along the sea coasts. Today, the Cormorant (*Phalacrocorax carbo*) is recorded as a common, overwintering bird in Bible lands; the Pygmy Cormorant (*Phalacrocorax pygmaeus*) is still, but very rarely, seen as a winter visitor; and the related Shag (*Phalacrocorax aristotelis*) is a very rare accidental.

CRANE

Crane (*Grus grus*)
(Photograph: Arthur Christiansen)

'Like a crane . . . so did I chatter.' (Isaiah 38:14)

There are two references to this bird, each figurative, relating to its voice and its migration: 'Like a crane or a swallow, so did I chatter: I did mourn as a dove: mine eyes fail with looking upward' (Isaiah 38:14); and 'Yea, the stork in heaven knoweth her appointed times; and the turtle and the crane and the swallow observe the time of their coming' (Jer 8:7).

The Hebrew word is *Aqur*, identified by modern zoologists as the genus *Grus*, the crane, which is known to have a distinctive voice and occurs in a Talmudic expression 'he shrieked like a crane'. The Common Crane (*Grus grus*) does migrate seasonally in Bible lands and its call can be heard at great distances when a flight is passing over. These great migrations must have been a magnificent sight in the quieter skies of Old Testament times as they headed south for the winter warmth of Africa from their breeding grounds across northern Europe. It is a tall bird, very much like a heron or a stork, although not related to either. It is mainly grey in body colour with a black head and black wing tips, a white stripe down the side of the neck and a bright red patch on top of the head. Its tail is hidden when it stands by a large tuft of plumes. Cranes inhabit mainly wetlands, living on a wide diet from grass and grain to insects and small mammals. They are today recorded as rare winter visitors, but during January are to be seen in large numbers migrating to the north.

Cuckoo

Only one reference, as a forbidden bird: 'And these are they which ye shall have in abomination ... and the cuckoo and the hawk after his kind' (Lev 11:13-16 and Deut 14:15).

The Hebrew word is *Shalaf* and the translation is in dispute. Modern zoologists think that it represents some member of the genus *Larus*, that is the gulls, and the modern versions all agree. There are, however, cuckoos in Bible lands, both the great spotted Cuckoo (*Clamator glandarius*) and the European cuckoo (*Cuculus canorus*) are regular visitors. Because of the cuckoo chick's habit of throwing out the eggs (or even the young) of its foster parents, it represents a powerful symbol in moral teaching and the AV translators had even stranger notions of its habits, as recorded in *Hortus Sanitatis*: 'They have their own time of coming and are born upon the wings of kites, because of their short and small flight, lest they be tired in the long tracts of air and die. From their spittle, grasshoppers are produced. In the winter it lies languishing and unfeathered, and looks like an owl.'

Cuckoo (*Cuculus canorus*)

DEER

Although the word 'deer' does not occur in the AV, there are references to 'hart' (eleven), 'hind' (ten)', 'roe and roebuck' (seventeen), and 'fallow deer' (two). Almost all the translations 'roebuck' are from the Hebrew word '*Tsebi*', which modern translators are agreed means 'GAZELLE' (q.v.). The rest could be to any or all of the three species of deer which once lived in Bible lands: the Red Deer, the Fallow Deer, and the Roe Deer. These were all allowed as food (Deut 12:15, 22; 14:15 and 15:22) and they appeared daily on Solomon's table (1 Kings 4:23). They were famous for their power of leaping (Isaiah 35:5) and weakness when deprived of food (Lam 1:6), or drink, when they pant for cooling streams (Psa 42:1). The hind was proverbially sure-footed (2 Sam 22:34; Psa 18:33 and Hab 3:19); her calving is at a time known to God but not, it is implied, to Job (Job 39:1); and it is recorded that she will desert her young when pasture becomes scarce (Jer 14:5), though this may well be a reference to the devotion of the hind in that only in an extremity of drought could things get so bad that the hind will desert her young.

The deer played a part, in Hebrew legend, in the deception of Isaac: at the time Esau was hunting, he would secure a deer and leave it bound while he looked for other game. Satan arrived as soon as he left. He liberated the deer and when Esau returned the deer was gone. Because this was repeated several times, the return of Esau from the hunt was delayed and Jacob was able to secure his father's blessing. Also in Hebrew legend the swiftness of the deer was proverbial and the last words addressed by Judah to his sons were to remind them that the Lord had granted to him such fleetness of foot that he could overtake the hind on the run and prepare it as a dish for his father. There is an echo of this in Napthali's last words to his children, in which he reminds them that he was so fleet of foot that he had been appointed his father's messenger and called by him the 'hind let loose'. There is also a Hebrew legend that Satan, disguised as a deer, once lured David, while hunting, deep into the territory of the Philistines where he was seized by the giant Ishbi, brother of Goliath, and cast into a wine press where he would have been squeezed to death if the earth had not opened miraculously to save him.

The AV translators may well have been acquainted with the deer's musical sensibilities as recorded in Topsell's *Four-footed Beasts*:

> Harts are deceived with music, for they so love that harmony that they forbear their food to follow it. They live very long – 2,112 years. The bones of young harts are applied for making of pipes, but if a young one be pricked in his leg with cactus, his bones will never make pipes. If men drink in pots wherein are wrought harts' horns, it will weaken all force of venom ... Orpheus, in his *Book of Stones*, commandeth a husband to carry about him a hart's horn if he will live in amity and concord with his wife.

The Red Deer (*Cervus elaphus*) is the biggest of the three species, reaching up to 150 cm at the shoulders. It lives in herds outside the rutting season in sexual separation, usually in woodland areas during the day and emerging to graze around the edges at night. Red Deer love to swim and to wallow in mud. They live for up to 15 years. But, although they were protected as a species for the royal hunt in many parts of the world because of their magnificent appearance, and some of the Egyptian temple illustrations seem to suggest that the Red Deer was hunted, they have long been extinct in Bible lands.

The Fallow Deer (*Dama dama*) is rather smaller, reaching only around 100 cm at the shoulders. The name is from an Old English word meaning pale reddish or brownish grey in colour, which accurately describes its appearance, although it is also characterised by having a dappled spotting along its back which other species lose as they reach maturity. This is very effective coloration when standing under a tree where the sunlight falls dappled through the leaves as shown in the photograph. They have now been hunted out of Bible lands.

The Roe Deer (*Capreolus capreolus*) is much smaller – around 75 cm only at the shoulder – and has a very distinctive white flash at the tail. It was once very widespread in the area, though driven up into the mountains by hunting where it could be seen against the skyline leaping among the rocks and providing a readily recognisable image of nimbleness. Roe Deer are territorial and the males drive away rivals from their territory, so they are more frequently seen alone than other species. The Roe Deer was the emblem of the tribe of Naphthali, whose land stretched along the hill country which overlooks the Hula valley in the north, but then it moved south and took refuge along the slopes of Mount Carmel. Today it is a rarity.

Red Deer (*Cervus elaphus*)

'Until the day break and the shadows flee away . . . be thou like a roe or a young hart upon the mountains . . . (Song of Solomon 2:17)

D OG

Mange dog (*Canus familiaris*)

'A living dog is better than a dead lion.' (Ecclesiastes 9:4)

When we consider the Bible references to the dog, we have to forget the notions that we may have developed in our own society of the loyal and intelligent friend to man who deserves our respect and affection. Dogs were indeed useful to men in Bible times; but either as scavengers, who cleared the village rubbish heaps of rotting flesh, or as guardians of the flocks. In both roles they were most effective if they were fierce and hungry. There is not even a certain reference to the Hunting Dogs which were familiar in Assyria (though see the entry GREYHOUND). Most OT references are clearly to the Pariah Dogs that were so familiar in the Bible lands. They went careering around the walls of the cities at night (Psa 59:6); it was very dangerous to interfere with them (Prov 26:17); they would devour even human bodies (1 Kings 14:12; 16:4; 21:3) and they would eat the flesh that men could not eat (Exod 22:31). Violent men are compared to them (Psa 22:16, 20), and the name of 'dog', meaning all that is cowardly, lazy, filthy, treacherous and contemptible, is the most extreme term of abuse (1 Sam 22:14; 2 Sam 3:8; 9:8; 16:9; 2 Kings 8:13; Isaiah 66:3).

The NT references include the admonition of Christ that we

must not give that which is holy to the dogs (Matt 7:6), and the story of the Canaanite woman who, on being told by Jesus that it is not right that the children's bread should be thrown to the dogs, replies that the dogs were allowed to eat the scraps that fall from the Master's table (Matt 15:26-7). Then there are the dogs which come to the gate of the rich man Dives to lick the sores of the poor man Lazarus (Luke 16:22) and the proverbial dog who returns to his own vomit (2 Peter 2:22). St Paul uses the dog as a term of abuse in Phil 3:2 and, in the final chapter of the Bible, dogs appear, cast out from the blessed city, in company with 'whoremongers and murderers and idolators and whosoever loveth and maketh a lie' (Rev 22:15).

So, all the way from Exodus to Revelations, dogs are abused in the Bible. And in Hebrew legend, the term 'dog' was a familiar name with which to abuse an enemy. There is a tale that the final indignity on the corpses of the Egyptians who were drowned at the closing of the Red Sea was that the Israelites were able to turn and see the dogs gnawing the feet that had kicked them. The dog was unable to remain continent on the Ark during the period of the Flood and was declared unclean, and Esau demonstrated the depths of his impiety by feeding to his blind father, in place of goat's meat, the flesh of a dog.

The AV translators would have shared the biblical distaste for dogs: Shakespeare never says a good word for them, and the time was much engaged by manoeuvres to guard against being barked at, or bitten, by dogs. Lupton gives this advice in his *A Thousand Notable Things*:

> The tongue of a dog laid under the great toe within the shoe doth cease the barking of dogs at the party that so wears the same. . . . If you pluck out one of the eyes of a black dog whiles he is living, and will carry it with you, it will make that no dogs shall bark at you: yea, though you walk among them. . . . The teeth of a mad dog that hath bitten a man or a woman, tied in leather and then hanged at the shoulder, doth preserve and keep the party that bears it, from being bitten of any mad dog.

The Pariah Dog is a subspecies of *Canis familiaris* and is said to have interbred with Jackals or with Wolves. They certainly resemble the Jackal in appearance, having short sharp ears and nose and a tawny coat. They live and hunt in packs, although each tends to have its own lair to which it returns to lie up during the day.

DOVE

Collared Dove
(*Streptopelia decoacto*)

'O my dove that art in the clefts of the rock, in the secret places of the stairs...' (Song of Solomon 2:14)

There are 31 references to dove and eleven to pigeon. It is by far the most important bird in the Bible. The two words are, in our own time, practically synonymous, and in the translations from the Hebrew, the same word is found variously as 'pigeon' or 'dove' so they can be treated together. The dove is one of the earliest birds to be mentioned in the Bible, it being sent out by Noah from the Ark three times, firstly to return, having found no resting place, and then, seven days later, to return with the olive branch in its mouth, a sign that the tops of the trees were uncovered. The third and final time it failed to return (Gen 8:8-12). It is known to be capable of distant flight (Psa 55-6), and it is beautiful and pure (Cant 1:15; 2:14; 4:1; 5:2; 5:12; 6:9), but its song can be mournful (Isaiah 38:14; 59:11) and its foolishness is used to illustrate the stupidity of Ephraim (Hos 7:11). The dove was the only sacrificial bird specified in Mosaic law and was widely used, particularly by the less well-to-do. It was prepared by Abraham when God showed His intention to bless him (Gen 15:9).

A certain time after the birth of a child, the mother was required to bring both a lamb and a young pigeon as an offering or, if she was too poor, she could bring two pigeons (Lev 12:6-8). In the New Testament, we learn that the mother of Jesus, being poor, availed herself of this provision (Luke 2:24). For the purification of a leper, two turtle doves or two pigeons were specified, one a sin offering and one a burnt offering (Lev 14:22).

Because pigeons and doves were so widely used in sacrifice, the merchants of the temple had stocks of them, which were scattered by Jesus (John 2:16). The Spirit of God descends upon Jesus in the shape of a dove (Matt 3:16), and the disciples are told to be 'as wise as serpents, and harmless as doves' (Matt 10:16). The dove was depicted on the standards of the Assyrians and the Babylonians, not as an emblem of peace but in honour of the goddess Semiramis who founded the empires and reigned for 42 years and then resigned her powers to her son, taking flight to heaven in the shape of a dove.

Although the dove was never worshipped by the Hebrews, it was not mentioned in the Old Testament as an article of diet, even though it is a 'clean' bird. The dove was the emblem of Israel, in its innocence, and over the throne of Solomon was set a dove with its claw resting on a hawk, as a token that the time would come when all the warring nations should be delivered to the hands of Israel. There is also a moral to be drawn, in Hebrew legend, from the life of the dove: it is monogamous and points the way for mankind.

There was a tradition in AV times, recorded by the naturalist Bartholomew, that the Turtle Dove was characterised by the most intense fidelity and chastity:

> ... if he loseth his mate, he seeketh not the company of any other, but goeth alone, and hath mind of the fellowship that is lost, and groaneth alway, and loveth and chooseth solitary places, and flieth much company of men. He cometh in Springtime and warneth of novelty of time with groaning voice.

There are two distinct groups of species of doves, or pigeons: the genus *Columba*, which includes the Wood Pigeon, Stock Dove and Rock Dove; and the genus *Streptopelia*, which includes the Turtle Dove and the Collared Dove. All five are found in Bible lands. The Wood Pigeon (*Columba palumbus*) is common during the winter months around the wooded areas, especially around the forests of Gilead, but it heads north in March and is the same species that is found in Europe. The Stock Dove (*Columba oenas*), which is rarer and can be distinguished by having no white flash on the neck or bars on the wings, is also a winter visitor. The Rock Dove (*Columba livia*), which is the ancestor of the domestic pigeons and looks rather like a modern racing pigeon with its slim, sleek outlines, lives in the rocky slopes of the valleys. The Turtle Dove (*Streptopelia turtur*), whose distinctive call is so reminiscent of its Latin species name, is smaller still, with a chestnut front and distinctive black tail. It is both a resident and passage migrant in Bible lands, occupying a wide range of habitats from open country and woodlands to farmlands and gardens. The slightly larger Collared Dove (*Streptopelia decaocto*), which is distinguished by the black half collar around its neck, has colonised even wider areas, including the towns and villages and is today the largest and the most successful of the *Streptopelia*.

E AGLE

There are 32 references to the most majestic of birds, mostly figurative uses as images of its unique qualities: its swiftness of flight (Deut 28:9; 2 Sam 1:23; Jer 4:13; 48:40; Lam 4:19; Job 9:26; Prov 23:5); its high soaring (Obad 4; Isaiah 4:30); and its habit of building a high and inaccessible nest (Jer 49:16). And, perhaps most intriguing of all from the natural history point of view, a behavioural note about the eagle's care and training of the young: 'As an eagle stirreth up her nest, fluttereth over her young, spreadeth abroad her wings, taketh them, beareth them on her wings' (Deut 32:11). This was taken by early commentators as an accurate eyewitness report of the habits of the eagle: that it would deliberately 'stir up' the nest to encourage the young fledglings to take to their wings, and that when they had left the nest, usually by climbing uncertainly out onto the surrounding rocks and branches, the mother would flutter over them to teach them to fly. She would even go to the lengths of taking them on her back and then flying far away from the trees and crags and tipping them off, to swoop down below and catch them on her wings, so gradually teaching them to fly. There is no modern record of this particular piece of behaviour, though it is very appealing and represents God's care for humanity in that He occasionally ruffles up our nests to persuade us into self-reliance, but is always ready to catch us as we fall. The image is repeated in

the words of the Lord to Moses when He describes his care for the children of Israel: 'I bare you on eagle's wings and brought you unto myself' (Exod 19:14). The baldness of the eagle in Micah 1:16 probably refers to the VULTURE (q.v.), either the Griffon, which has a head and neck covered in white down and so looks unfeathered at a distance, or the Lappet-faced, which has head and neck covered in bare red skin.

Golden Eagle (*Aquila chrysaetos*)

'I bare you on eagle's wings and brought you unto myself.' (Exodus 19:4)

There is also the reference to the renewal of youth 'like the eagle's' (Psa 103:5) which may refer to the early belief that the eagle, when old, would one day soar high into the air and then plunge straight down into the sea and so renew his plumage. But the Egyptian phoenix was transformed, in early Christian art, into the eagle and then used as a symbol of the resurrection because of the legend of its plunging into fire and then arising, new-born, from the ashes.

There is a Hebrew tale which records the power and longevity of the eagle: it is said that Solomon, one day, found a magnificent building, into which he could not enter because there seemed to be no door. He came across the eagle, 700 years old, and asked where the door might be. The eagle could not tell, but sent the king to visit its elder brother, who was 900 years old, and whose eyrie was higher than his own. The brother could not help but sent Solomon to his still older brother who was 1,300 years old and who said that he could remember his father saying there was a door on the west side.

The king found the great iron door all hidden by the dust of ages and on it an inscription: 'We, the dwellers in this palace, for many years lived in comfort and in luxury; then forced by hunger, we ground pearls into flour instead of wheat – but to no avail and so, when we were about to die, we bequeathed this place to the eagles.'

The eagle became the emblem of St John the Evangelist because of the acuity of its vision and the fitting comparison that, as John was able to gaze on the Holy Spirit for inspiration, so the eagle was able to strengthen its eyes by gazing at the sun. The AV translators would have been made aware of this habit by the naturalist Bartholomew who wrote:

> She taketh her own birds in her claws and maketh them to look on the sun, and that ere their wings be full grown, and except they look stiffly and steadfastly towards the sun, she beateth them and setteth them even tofore the sun [sic]; and if the eye of any of her birds watereth on looking on the sun, she slayeth him.

This habit is also recorded in Pliny.

Most modern commentators have agreed with Canon Tristram that the references to the eagle, which use the Hebrew word *Nesher*, cognate with the Arabic *Nissr*, mean not the eagle but the Griffon Vulture. But it would be very hard to differentiate between these birds of prey as they soar high out of reach on the clouds and build their nests in inaccessible peaks, so precise identification is difficult and the eagle was certainly the more familiar in folklore. Even the reference of Christ 'wheresoever the carcase is, there will the eagles be gathered together' (Matt 24:28), which the modern versions translate as 'vultures', could well mean literally the eagle (Greek *aetos*) since eagles, as well as vultures, eat carrion.

The eagles in Bible lands today are mainly migrants or overwintering birds. The Golden Eagle (*Aquila chrysaetos*), the large, dark, mainly silent majestically soaring figure which stays for hours on the wing and inhabits the highest reaches of the mountain tops, calls occasionally; the slightly smaller Bonelli's Eagle (*Hieraaetus fasciatus*), with its spotted white under-feathers, is at home here; and the much smaller Short-toed Eagle (*Circaetus gallicus*), which is also called the Snake eagle from its habit of eating snakes, and rather like a large, white buzzard in flight, does well. The Imperial Eagle (*Aquila heliaca*), distinguished by the white patches on its scapulars, is a winter visitor and passage migrant from southeast Europe.

F ALLOW DEER

There are two references quite specifically to the Fallow, as distinct from other deer. In Deuteronomy, the animal is specified as permitted food: 'These are the beasts which ye shall eat . . . the hart and the roebuck and the fallow deer' (Deut 14:4-5). And, in the context of the magnificent provisions of Solomon, interestingly the meat entries follow the permitted list: 'And Solomon's provision for one day was . . . ten fat oxen . . . and an hundred sheep . . . besides hart and roebuck and fallow deer' (1 Kings 4:22-3).

The Hebrew word used here is *Jahmur*, which modern zoologists have identified as *Dama dama*, the Fallow deer, and there is evidence that the Persian Fallow Deer (*Dama dama mesopotamica*) featured on the menu of the Carmel cave dwellers. But it had disappeared from the area before the Roe deer and modern translators prefer, in these passages, either the Roebuck or the Roe deer (see entry under DEER.)

Persian Fallow Deer (*Dama dama mesopotamica*)

FERRET

Only mentioned once, in the list of forbidden meats of Leviticus: 'These also shall be unclean unto you among the creeping things that creep upon the earth ... and the ferret and the chameleon' (Lev 11:29-30). The Hebrew word is *Anaka* and its interpretation has given trouble to Bible scholars. The old Greek translation has it as 'shrew mouse' and indeed there are shrews to be found in Bible lands. The Rabbinical writers prefer 'hedgehog', which is also common, but perhaps is not properly described as a 'creeping thing'. All the modern translators have settled on GECKO (q.v.).

FLEA

Dog Flea
(*Ctenocephalides canis*)
(Photograph:
Larry West)

'For the King of Israel is
come out to seek a
flea ...' (1 Sam 24:14)

In two contexts, in both of which it is an image for something pursued: 'After whom is the King of Israel come out? after whom dost thou pursue? after a dead dog, after a flea?' (1 Sam 24:14). And later: 'for the King of Israel is come out to seek a flea, as when one doth hunt a partridge in the mountains' (1 Sam 26:20). Here the image is plainly meant to convey something small and insignificant and unworthy of the attention of the king.

The Hebrew word is *Parosh*, identified by modern zoologists as *Pulex irritans*, the so-called 'human flea', which is also a parasite of foxes, Badgers and other hole-dwelling animals. The flea does not figure largely in Hebrew legend, although there is the story that, in the war with the Ninevites, Judah said one day to Jacob that he should rest and let his son fight the battle, whereupon Judah hopped and jumped over the opposing army like a flea, from one warrior to the next, until he had killed 8,096 men, whereupon fatigue overcame him. So the image was part of Hebrew consciousness.

The AV translators had a very interesting notion of the value of the conduct of the flea as helping the prognosis of disease. In *A Thousand Notable Things* Lupton writes:

When any draws nigh toward their death, and their members lack blood and vital heat: then fleas and lice leave them quite, or else draw to that part of the body where the said heat tarries the longest; which is in the hole in the neck under the chin, etc. This is a token that death is at hand.

Pulex irritans is said not to have been introduced to man until he became a cave-dweller, when he picked it up from the other animals which were already cave-dwellers. Although, as the Hebrews recorded, it is a notable jumper and has been known to leap up to 30 cm, it prefers to scuttle along the surface of the skin, helped by strong claws that can get a grip of the hairs and backward pointing bristles that keep it from slipping down a vertical surface. The female flea lays several hundred eggs at a time, often on the host, and these develop after a week or two into white, worm-like larvae, having neither heads nor eyes, but simply biting jaws which enable them to live off the detritus around the nest. Adult fleas need a stimulus of some kind to enable them to emerge from the cocoon, and this is provided by a vibration or movement from the body of a living animal. This is a handy arrangement, because if they happen to be situated on an animal which has died, they can remain in cocoon until a living animal comes along on which they can feed. This trait in flea behaviour explains why some houses that have been left vacant for some time can become 'alive with fleas' as soon as somebody moves in and starts shifting the furniture around.

F LY

Mentioned twice. The first is in a proverbial context which we still make use of: 'Dead flies cause the ointment of the apothecary to send forth a stinking savour' (Eccl 10:1) – whence our phrase 'a fly in the ointment'. And then there is the phrase 'The Lord shall hiss for the fly that is in the uttermost part of the rivers of Egypt' (Isaiah 7:18) where the context suggests that the Lord will whistle up a plague of some kind, of stinging or biting flies that will attack His enemies. The Hebrew word used here is *Zebub* which is still known in the name Beelzebub, the Lord of the Flies, applied in the time of Christ to the prince of the devils (Matt 12:24).

It would be consistent with the Old Testament practice in which God uses natural means to affect His purpose that the Lord should call up a plague of flies and, indeed, there was the plague referred to in Exodus 8, in which the biblical text omits the word 'flies' (in the AV it is printed in italics to indicate this). But the clear reference in Psa 78:45 and 105:31 to the plague of flies confirms the use of the word in Exodus. Here the Hebrew is *Arob*, which is most probably a biting midge or mosquito. The family *Ceratopogonidae*, known in some parts of America as 'No-see-ums', seems quite possible.

F OX

There is a great deal about the proverbial and the natural behaviour of the fox in the Bible references. Its fondness for grapes, as recorded in the well-known fable, occurs in 'Take us the foxes, the little foxes, that spoil the vines: for our vines have tender grapes' (S. of S. 2:15). The solitary wandering as well as the native wisdom of the fox are what lead Ezekiel to the comparison 'O Israel thy prophets are like foxes in the deserts' (Ezek 13:14). That foxes inhabited ruins in Bible times is shown in 'Because of the mountain of Zion which is desolate, the foxes walk upon it' (Lam 5:18) and 'Even that which they build if a

fox go up he shall break down their stone wall' (Neh 4:3). And the best known of all: 'the foxes have holes and the birds of the air have nests: but the Son of Man hath nowhere to lay his head' (Matt 8:20 and Luke 9:58).

Fennec Fox
(*Fennecus zerda*)

'Take us the foxes, the little foxes, that spoil the vines.' (Song of Solomon 2:15)

The other New Testament reference is to the malign cunning of Herod: 'Go tell that fox, behold, I cast out devils' (Luke 13:32). There is also a pair of texts which commentators seem agreed should refer to the Jackal: 'They shall fall by the sword: they shall be a portion for foxes' (Psa 63:10), on the ground that the Jackal is the scavenger of Bible lands, and the story of Samson catching 300 foxes and then tying firebrands to their tails and loosing them amid the corn (Judges 15), where it is held that, since foxes go about alone or in pairs, it would have been impossible for Samson to have caught 300 of them, whereas Jackals go in packs and the incident would be more credible. This is to carry our need for rational explanations into improper areas: there are many feats of Samson which go beyond the probable and there is no need to change a translation in order to make this one more acceptable to us today.

The Hebrew word is *Shual*, which can be identified with the Red Fox, and possibly a local subspecies, *Vulpes vulpes niloticus*, which exists in the area today. There is also a Hebrew legend which records the cunning of the fox in which it is said that, after the sin of Adam, God gave the world up into the power of the Angel of Death, with the command that he should cast a pair of each kind of animal into the waters. When the Angel of Death took hold of the fox, he began to weep bitterly and said he was lamenting the fate of his friend who had been cast into the water, pointing to his own reflection. Satisfied, the Angel of Death let him go.

The fox of Bible lands is possibly slightly greyer than the red European version, having yellowish-brown fur on the back and a slate-grey belly. The backs of its ears are black. It is very widely distributed from the snows of Mount Hermon to the basalt plains of the Golan, in the woods of Galilee and the Judaean mountains, and also in the towns and villages.

Grapes are not normally part of the fox's diet; it lives on a wide range of foods from earthworms to partridges and hares and will also eat grass, carrion, and any leftover meals in urban dustbins. Foxes have litters, in the early spring, of up to six cubs.

F ROG

When the Pharaoh refused to let the people go, one of the plagues visited on his land was that of the frogs which swarmed all over Egypt. This incident, recorded in Exodus, Chapter 8, is the only context in which frogs occur in the Old Testament. The plague is also recalled in Psalms 78:45 and 105:30. In the New Testament there is also only one reference to frogs: the unclean spirits, the workers of false miracles which came out of the mouth of the dragon, were 'like frogs' (Rev 16:13).

The Hebrew word is *Tsefardea*, which modern zoologists identify as the genus *Rana*, the great group of true frogs which are found just about everywhere. Some suggest that the species could well have been *Rana esculenta*, the Edible Frog, but there is no evidence for this, other than that this is very common in Bible lands today. The Greek word used in Revelations is *Batrachos*.

The frog has a very mixed image in Hebrew legend. At the

Edible Frog (*Rana esculenta*)

'He sent . . . frogs which destroyed them.' (Psalm 78:45)

Creation, the Lord deprived it of teeth so that it would not threaten other animals in the water; on the other hand the frog is the model for self-sacrifice since it offers itself as food to starving aquatic creatures in fulfilment of the injunction 'if thine enemy be hungry, give him bread to eat'. The frog had magical powers and was exceedingly wise: it was a frog who taught the Rabbi Hanina the whole of the Torah, the 70 languages of men and the speech of birds and mammals by writing the words on scraps of paper and making his pupil swallow them. The plague of frogs is commemorated today in that the crocodiles of the Nile are descended from the frogs that God sent as a plague to Egypt.

In the times of the AV the frog was thought to be both magical and venomous and was a frequent ingredient in witches' broth. Topsell, in his *History of Serpents*, also grants them medicinal virtues: 'The flesh of Frogs is good against the biting of the sea hare, the scorpion, and all kinds of serpents. The broth taken into the body with the roots of the sea holm expelleth the salamander.' And Albertus Magnus writes in his book *Of the Wonders of the World* of an intriguing but infallible purpose to which the frog might be put: 'That a woman may confess what she has done, catch a live water frog and take out its tongue and put the frog back into the water and put the tongue over the region of the woman's heart while she is asleep, and, when she is questioned, she will tell the truth.'

The Edible Frog is, although to some people unpleasant to touch and slimy in appearance, beautifully coloured with bright green speckled back and eyes spangled with gold. They are found all over the Bible lands, wherever there is marsh or water, and their croaking, especially at night, makes them one of the most evident presences in the animal world.

GAZELLE

Dorcas Gazelle
(*Gazella dorcas*)

'Make haste, my beloved, and be thou like to a roe or to a young hart among the mountains of spices.' (Song of Solomon 8:14)

Although the name does not occur in the Old Testament, this omission can be explained linguistically in that the word is first recorded in English, as an introduction from the Arabic, in 1600 and it may well have been too recent an introduction for the AV translators to have taken account of. There is general agreement today that the Hebrew word *Tsebi*, which has an Arabic cognate *Zabi*, meaning gazelle, should be so translated and not, as in the AV, 'Roe' or 'Roebuck'. The gazelle is expressly permitted as food (Deut 12:15; 14:5; 15:22) and was duly served at the table of Solomon (1 Kings 4:23). It is used in imagery as when Asahel, brother of Joab, is described as being as light of foot as a gazelle (2 Sam 2:18) and the Gadites, who came to join David in the wilderness, were as swift upon the mountains (1 Chron 12:8). Gazelles, the most charming of the antelopes, are frequently mentioned in the Song of Songs (2:7; 2:9, 3:5; 8:14).

Hebrew lore has it that the gazelle is under the special protection of God. It gives birth to its young on the topmost pinnacle of a rock to which God sends the eagle to catch up the young and return it to its mother before it can slip to its death. The timidity of the gazelle is also a fitting image of the response of the world to the anger of the Lord (Isaiah 13:14).

The name Tabitha, and its Greek form Dorcas, which mean gazelle, are both popular for girls in Bible lands as being redolent of the grace and beauty of the gazelle. *Gazella dorcas* roams the high plateaux of the Holy Lands in herds of from five to ten, feeding on artemisia and steppe grass. In Canon Tristram's day they were also found on the edges of the deserts and the grey hills of Galilee, and even sharing the rocks of Engedi with wild goats. In the company of the sheikhs, he witnessed the hunting of the gazelle using both greyhound and falcon. Today, with more intensive hunting and the easy availability of firearms, the population has been much reduced.

GECKO

Another word that does not occur in the AV but, because translators from the RV onwards are agreed that it is the correct rendering of the Hebrew *Anaka*, rendered 'ferret' in the AV version of Leviticus 11:30, and because the word did not enter the English vocabulary before 1774 it may be accepted in that context. There is also a Hebrew word *Smamit*, rendered 'spider' in the AV, which most modern translators render

Fan-footed Gecko
(*Ptyodactylus
hasselquisti*)

'The lizard which you
can catch in your hand,
yet it frequents the
palaces of kings.'
(Proverbs 30:28. J.B.)

'lizard'. The context, however, strongly suggests the gecko: 'The lizard, which you can catch in your hand, yet it frequents the palaces of kings' (Prov 30:28), JB.

By far the most likely lizard to be found in the palaces of kings, or for that matter in any building, is the gecko, so often seen today walking up walls or across ceilings. They are the most agile climbers of the lizard family, their widespread toes being broad and fleshy and having folds of skin on the inner surfaces which allow them to adhere, even to glass. Most geckos are active at night and have specially adapted eyesight with a vertical slit in the iris. Geckos lay eggs, but not prolifically: some lay only two, some just one. They are easy to catch in the hand and are often raised as children's pets.

 GIER

Mentioned only in the list of forbidden birds: 'These are they which ye shall have in abomination ... the swan and the pelican and the gier eagle' (Lev 11:13-18 and Deut 14:17). Because the Hebrew word *Raham* is found only in this context, it has proved difficult to identify, and the word 'gier', used by the AV translators, is found today only in such combinations as

Gyr Falcon and Lammergeier. All modern authorities are agreed that some sort of vulture is intended and modern Israeli zoologists suggest the Egyptian Vulture (*Neophron percnopterus*). (See VULTURE.)

Egyptian Vulture at Red Deer carcase (*Neophron percnopterus*)

GLEDE

Another textual problem in that this word is found only in the list of forbidden birds: 'But these are they of which ye shall not eat . . . and the glede and the kite and the vulture after his kind' (Deut 14:12-13). The name glede, which is found only in the AV, was used in England as a regional name for the kite, the osprey, the buzzard and the Peregrine Falcon. Modern versions of the Bible are divided between the kite and the buzzard (see KITE.)

Buzzard (*Buteo buteo*)

G NAT

The only mention of this creature is in the well-known words of Christ: 'Ye blind guides, which strain at a gnat and swallow a camel' (Matt 23:24). The phrase was changed in the RV to 'strain out a gnat', being a return to the translations of Tyndale Cranmer and the Geneva Bible, and the modern translators have followed suit, referring the phrase to the practice of strict Jews of straining their wine through a cloth in order to avoid drinking any small insects which may have fallen in. This is in conformity with the injunction declaring flying, creeping things to be unclean (Lev 11:23). There is an interesting parallel with this in the Arabic proverb 'he eats an elephant and is suffocated by a gnat'.

In Hebrew legend, the gnat is known as a feeble creature which takes in food but never excretes it; the gnat is also known as a specific remedy for the poison of the viper. It is a reminder to man of his relatively late appearance on earth and an admonition to humility, since God created the gnat before man. And it is an example of how the most insignificant of God's creatures can have a mission to carry out: it lives for only one day, but it was a gnat that managed to kill Titus Flavius Vespasianus, destroyer of Jerusalem, by crawling up his nose and into his brain.

The word gnat is one of those which have a different meaning in Britain and America. The British use it to indicate a small fly of the genus *Culex*, especially *Culex pipiens*, whereas in America it means simply the mosquito, *Culex mosquito*. The latter is still very prevalent in Bible lands.

Gnat (*Culex pipiens*)

'Ye blind guides, which strain at a gnat, and swallow a camel.' (Matthew 23:24)

GOAT

There are 124 references to the Domestic Goat, using six Hebrew and two Greek words, all reflecting the important place that this animal had and still has in the lives of the inhabitants of the Bible lands. Goats were an important indicator of wealth: Laban had large flocks (Gen 30:33); Jacob gave 200 she-goats and 20 he-goats to Esau (Gen 32:14); Nabal had 1,000 goats (1 Sam 25:2). Kids, especially, were used as food (Gen 27:9; Judges 6:19; 13:15; Luke 15:29), though it was specifically forbidden to seethe them in their mothers' milk (Exod 23:19). Goat milk was a popular drink (Prov 27:27) and the bottles in which wine was kept were made of goat skins (Jos 9:4; Mark 2:22), as occasionally were clothes (Heb 11:37). Goat hair was used for stuffing pillows (1 Sam 19:13) and woven to form a covering for the Tabernacle (Exod 26:7). Above all, goats were used for sacrifices.

With all of these valuable attributes, the goat must have been highly prized and goat keepers today might well wonder why

Wild Goat (*Capra aegagrus*)

'And thou shalt have goats milk, enough for thy food . . .' (Proverbs 27:27)

Christ seems to have held such a poor view of them, separating them from the sheep and then sending them, albeit figuratively, to eternal punishment (Matt 25:33). The ecological explanation is that the goats, unlike sheep, destroy the pastures they feed on by browsing so intensively that they make a desert of any fertile land to which they are allowed unrestricted access. Although this has been suggested by Bible scholars, it hardly rings true since sheep graze equally intensively: 'the greatest enemy a sheep has is another sheep', and will destroy pasture land as efficiently as goats. More probable is the explanation that contrasts the temperament of the two animals: the goat is always strongly individualistic, not to say wayward, whereas the sheep is docile and passive and easily led, a more fitting image of the meek who shall inherit the earth by recognising and obeying the voice of the ·Master.

The special significance of the goat to the Hebrews is that it was a goat skin which enabled Jacob to secure his father's blessing; the constellation Capricornus is a constant reminder of their indebtedness to the animal. Also the blood of a kid, which resembles human blood, was smeared by the brothers of Joseph on his coat of many colours in order to deceive his father into thinking he had been torn by wild beasts. This is why a kid was sacrificed, in atonement, at the dedication of the Tabernacle. And a golden goat stood, with a leopard, on the third step of the throne of Solomon.

Goats were said to have many miraculous virtues in AV times. Topsell's *Four-footed Beasts* records:

There is no beast that heareth so perfectly and so sure as a goat, for he is not only holp in this sense with his ears, but also hath the organ of hearing in part of his throat. With goat's milk, wine is preserved from corruption by sourness. Of the suet and fat of goats are the best candles made, because it is hard and not over-liquid. The blood of a goat scoureth rusty iron better than a file. The lodestone draweth iron, and the same, being rubbed with garlic, dieth, and loseth that property, but, being dipped again in goat's blood, reviveth and recovereth the former nature.

And Topsell's final note recognises the waywardness of the most individualistic of domestic animals: 'Goats love singularity and may well be called schismatics among cattle.'

The main ancestor of the Domestic Goat (*Capra hircus*) was probably the wild goat of the Caucasus (*Capra aegagrus*). (See WILD GOAT.)

GRASSHOPPER

There are nine references, all in the Old Testament, to the timidity, the smallness of stature, and yet the multiplicity of the grasshopper. It is permitted food: 'Ye may eat ... the grasshopper after his kind' (Lev 11:22); 'They came as grasshoppers for multitude' (Judges 6:5) and 'all the children of the east lay along the valley like grasshoppers for multitude' (Judges 7:12); and again, 'because they ate more than the grasshoppers and are innumerable' (Jer 46:23). And yet they are insignificant in size: 'and there we saw the giants ... and we were, in our own sight, as grasshoppers' (Num 13:33) and 'It is

Grasshopper (*Truxalis grandis*)

'And the grasshopper shall be a burden.' (Ecclesiastes 12:5)

71

he that sitteth upon the circle of the earth, and the inhabitants thereof are as grasshoppers' (Isaiah 40:22). And easily afrighted: 'Hast thou given the horse strength? ... Canst thou make him afraid as a grasshopper?' (Job 39:19-20). The most famous, and yet the most enigmatic text is, of course, that in Ecclesiastes: 'and the almond tree shall flourish, and the grasshopper shall be a burden, and desire shall fail' (Eccl 12:5).

Here the burden of the grasshopper is the sign of old age and commentators have long wrestled with precisely what is meant by the image. Some thought that Solomon is comparing the body of an old man with that of the grasshopper, because in age the body is dry and shrivelled, the bones obtrude, the knees project. Others have noted the fact that the grasshopper is permitted food and have suggested that, in old age, perhaps even a single insect can be too much of a burden for the shrunken appetite. Yet others have thought that, as in old age the slightest pressures or tensions are too much to bear, the preacher is saying that extra burdens, in old age, be they as light and as delicate as an insect, are intolerable. And some of the modern translations, attempting to throw light on the passage, have changed it to 'the grasshopper drags himself along', implying that, in old age, even an insect as nimble as a grasshopper is crippled by the passing years and reduced to a hobbling gait. The passage remains obscure and yet charged with poetic meaning.

In Hebrew legend the grasshopper, like the rest of the animal kingdom, has a lesson for man: all day long, all summer through, it sings and sings until eventually its belly bursts and death claims it. Although it knows the fate that awaits it, still it sings. So man should do his duty to God with cheerful heart, no matter what the consequences.

For the AV translators, grasshoppers were suspected of being portents of the future who had an unusually strong attachment to their place of birth. Mouffet records, in his *Theatre of Insects*:

They never alter their place, or at least very seldom; or if they do they are ever after silent; they sing no more; so much doth the love of their native soil prevail with them ... The Grasshoppers abounding in the end of spring do foretell a sickly year to come. Oftentimes their coming and singing doth portend the happy state of things. What year few of them are to be seen, they presage dearness of victuals, and scarcity of all things else.

The Hebrew word *Arbeh* has been identified by modern zoologists with the Locust (*Schistocerca gregaria*) and there is confusion in the usage of these names in everyday speech today. In America locust and grasshopper are almost interchangeable, whereas in Britain the grasshoppers are the smaller members of the order *Orthoptera* (straight-winged), which tend to live in a solitary fashion or in small communities, as opposed to the LOCUSTS (q.v.), which migrate in enormous hordes.

Grasshoppers are more often seen than heard, their coloration usually making them invisible in their surroundings. The 'song' is produced by drawing the leg against the wing-case, the leg having a number of ridges on it which strike the edge of the wing in turn, producing vibrations by the process known as stridulation, like drawing the teeth of a comb across the edge of a piece of card. Different species have different songs and those who are experts on grasshoppers find it easier to identify them by the pitch, volume and duration of their stridulation than by sight, just as many bird-watchers are better at recognition by birdsong than by the appearance of the bird.

GREYHOUND

Occurs only in one context: 'There be three things which go well, yea four which are comely in going ... A greyhound, an he-goat also, and a king against whom there is no rising up' (Prov 30:29-31).

The Hebrew word is *Zarzir*, which means literally tied, or girded in the loins. And some early commentators have thought the reference must be to the warhorse, ornamented about the loins with girth and buckles, as shown on the sculptures at Persepolis. Others have held it to be the wild ass of Abyssinia, which has striped skin on its loins giving it the appearance of being girded. Yet others have thought it to be a wrestler.

The modern translators are mostly in favour of 'strutting cock' (so NIV, NEB, GNB, NAS and JB); but AB has 'war horse' and RAV has preserved the AV 'greyhound' in the text with a footnote that admits 'exact identity unknown'.

H ARE

The only context is that of the list of unclean animals: 'And the hare, because he cheweth the cud but divideth not the hoof; he is unclean unto you' (Lev 11:6).

The Hebrew word is *Arnabet* and there is no argument about the identification, though natural historians have been quick to point out that the hare does not, in fact, chew the cud and therefore is improperly listed here as unclean. Canon Tristram explained that hares have the habit of grinding their teeth in order to keep them at the same length and that this gives them the appearance of chewing the cud. Since Moses speaks of animals according to their appearances and not with the precision of a comparative anatomist, it was reasonable to use the phrase 'chew the cud' since that is what the hare appears to be doing. Modern commentators have pointed to the hare's recently recorded habit of 'refection', that is the eating again of droppings which have passed through the body once so as to extract more completely the nourishment. This means that hares are frequently seen chewing, although not taking green stuff into their mouths.

In Hebrew mythology, the hare had magical powers, the most remarkable of which was the ability to change its sex. This was because the female hare had escaped from the Ark and drowned so that, when the Ark came to rest on Mount Ararat, only the male hare came out. And God gave him the power to bear children. Because of this ability, the stomach of a male hare was thought to be a cure for sterility, and this was the cure suggested to Samson's mother, against which the angel warns her in Judges 13:7. It was also said that Zedekiah was able to exercise power over Nebuchadnezzar because he had one day surprised Nebuchadnezzar in the act of cutting a piece of flesh from a live hare and eating it, according to the habit of the barbarians.

The Hebrew legends were a part of the folklore of the AV translators, as Topsell records in his *Four-footed Beasts*: 'A Hare is a four-footed beast of the earth which the Hebrews call *Arnabet* in the feminine gender, which word gave occasion to an opinion that all Hares were females, or, at the least, that the males bring forth young as well as females... The common sort of people suppose that they are one year male, and another female.' It was also thought that a person could

develop a hare lip from looking at a hare and desiring its flesh. And the natural historian Lupton writes that 'With its brains boys' gums are cleansed; for it has the power to make the teeth come quickly and without pain.'

Hares were often depicted on the wall paintings of Egypt and the hunting of hares is a popular theme in Assyrian seals and reliefs. The hare of Bible lands is a subspecies of the European Hare, *Lepus capensis*, which is slightly smaller and paler in colour than the European hare. It lives on in the grassy lowlands, giving birth to up to four leverets at a time in the 'forms', or nests which hares make above ground.

Desert Hare (*Lepus europeus syriacus*) (Photograph: Ofer Bahat)

'And the hare because he cheweth the cud but divideth not the hoof . . .' (Leviticus 11:6)

HAWK

Lesser Kestrel (*Falco naumanni*) and Sparrow-hawk (*Accipiter nisus*)

'Doth the hawk fly by thy wisdom.' (Job 39:26)

Mentioned twice: once in the list of birds which 'ye shall have in abomination ... the cuckoo and the hawk after his kind' (Lev 11:13-16 and Deut 14:15), where the intention is obviously to include all the smaller birds of prey collectively known by this name, and again in the lilting poetry of Job: 'Doth the hawk fly by thy wisdom and stretch her wings toward the South', where the meaning can be either that the smaller hawks tend to be migratory in Bible lands or, perhaps more fancifully, it has been suggested, a reference to the legend that the hawks had the power of flying, undazzled, straight into the eye of the sun.

The Hebrew word is *Netz*, which has been identified as including several of the smaller birds of prey such as the Kestrel (*Falco tinnunculus*) or the Hobby (*Falco subbuteo*). In common English usage, the word 'hawk' refers to any of the diurnal birds of prey which are used in falconry. In natural history parlance it usually refers to one of the species of the genus *Accipiter*, which is the largest genus of birds of prey in the world and includes the Sparrowhawk (*Accipiter nisus*), the Goshawk (*Accipiter gentilis*) and the Levant Sparrowhawk (*Accipiter brevipes*).

Hawks were commonly used in Hebrew legend as symbols of swiftness of flight and keenness of vision. The AV translators knew them as participants in the most intensely followed sport of the age: falconry. Shakespeare's writings are shot through with images from falconry and the laws of the land contained statutes passed from the time of William the Conqueror to guard its interest. Falcons and hawks were even allotted degrees and status corresponding to the rank and station of those who used them, as the eagle to the emperor, the Gyrfalcons to kings, the Peregrine to an earl, the Goshawk to a yeoman, the Sparrowhawk to a priest and the Kestrel to a knave or servant. That the hawks were by nature diurnal feeders is confirmed by *Hortus Sanitatis*, which records that they would refuse to eat any prey seized by chance after sunset: 'The Hawk holds beneath its talons all night a bird that fortune offers it at night time, but when the sun rises up, the hawk, even though hungry, lets the bird fly away, and if he meets it at some other time, does not pursue it.'

Of the hawks proper, the Sparrowhawk is recorded as a winter visitor and passage migrant, the Goshawk is occasionally seen as a straggler, and the smaller Shikra (*Accipiter badius*), from the south Caspian region, is a passage migrant. There is a rich variety of falcons, both resident and migrant, including the large Peregrine (*Falco peregrinus*) and Lanner (*Falco biarmicus*), as well as the smaller Sooty Falcon (*Falco concolor*) on the Red Sea coast and the Red-Footed Falcon (*Falco vespertinus*), the Kestrel and the Lesser Kestrel (*Falco naumanni*). With all this variety, it seems best to accept the word 'hawk' as meaning any one of the smaller birds of prey and not to attempt to tie it down to any specific species. The modern translators settle for the general phrase 'the hawk after his kind'.

H EN

Found only once, and that in the well-known anguished words of Christ in the New Testament: 'O Jerusalem, Jerusalem, thou killest the prophets and stonest them which are sent unto thee, how often would I have gathered thy children together, even as a hen gathereth her chickens under her wings, and ye would not!' (Matt 23:37 and Luke 13:34).

The Greek word is *Ornis* and it is surprising that a bird so intimately connected with the household and so common in Bible lands should occur only once in the Bible. There are echoes of the image in the psalmists' words 'hide me under the shadow of thy wings' (Psa 17:8), and perhaps also, 'He shall cover thee with his feathers, and under his wings shalt thou trust' (Psa 91:4).

There was a tale in AV times, recorded by the naturalist Bartholomew, that the devotion of a hen for her chickens was so intense as to cause her to lose her feathers and her voice: 'A Hen is a mild bird about chickens; for she taketh sickness for sorrow of her chickens and loseth her feathers. And her kindly love about her chickens is known by roughness of feathers and by harshness of voice.' The picture of the protective hen with her brood, under constant fear of threats from predators, gathering them under the warmth and comfort of her wings, must have been familiar to all who heard these words of Jesus.

Hen with chicks
(*Gallus domesticus*)
(Photograph: Ronald Thompson)

'O Jersusalem, Jerusalem . . . how often would I have gathered thy children together, even as a hen gathereth her chickens . . .
(Matthew 23:37)

HERON

Purple Heron (*Ardea purpurea*)

'... ye shall have in abomination among the fowls ... the heron after her kind ... (Leviticus 11:13-19)

Only one mention, in the list of unclean birds: 'And these are they which ye shall have in abomination among the fowls ... the stork, and the heron after her kind' (Lev 11:13-19).

The Hebrew word is *Anafa*, identified today as of the family *Ardeidae*, which includes the herons, egrets and bitterns. Clearly the phrase is meant to include a number of species of like birds which resemble the stork. In Hebrew legend the stork was a pious animal, so called because of its kindness and family loyalty; the heron, on the other hand, was unkind. Its name means 'the wrathful one' and it shared with the Ostrich the habit of neglecting its young. It had, in common with the stork, very keen sight and could see, from Babylon, any object in Palestine. The AV translators would have known herons as the chief prey of falconry, known for their cowardice as they flew high to escape the hawks. A dish of herons was presented to Edward III – cowardly birds for the cowardly king who dare not invade France.

There are ten species of heron in Bible lands, from the Goliath Heron (*Ardea goliath*), which is almost four feet tall, to the Little Bittern (*Ixobrychus minutus*), which grows to only 14 inches. The three most commonly seen are the Grey Heron (*Ardea cinerea*), the Night Heron (*Nycticorax nycticorax*) and the Purple Heron (*Ardea purpurea*). All are migrants and settle in shallow waters on the edges of rivers or lakes, marshes, estuaries and even ponds where they can find their diet of fish, water voles, mice, rats and young wildfowl.

HOOPOE

Found only in the list of unclean birds in Leviticus (11:19) and not so translated in the AV, which has 'Lapwing'. But the RV, the RSV and all modern versions have corrected to 'Hoopoe' and, since it is a rare bird in England and its name only became current in the seventeenth century, its absence from the AV is explained. Modern Israeli zoologists agree that 'Hoopoe' is correct.

The Hoopoe was a sacred bird to the Egyptians, which would account for its being an abomination to the Hebrews, but there was an additional, hygienic disincentive to eating it: the surroundings of its nest are always fouled by its droppings and the bird itself is often seen around the rubbish tips probing the detritus of human habitations for worms. There is an Arabic legend that its crest was a reward from Solomon for shielding him in the desert; and the Hoopoe is also credited, in Hebrew legend, with bringing to him the *shamir*, a special worm, insect, or perhaps stone (different legends identify it differently) which enabled him to shape the stones of the

Hoopoe (*Upupa epops*)

temple without using hammers or axes (1 Kings 6:7). The shamir was made by God on the sixth day of creation and placed under the guardianship of the Hoopoe. It was as large as a barleycorn and so hard that it would cut diamonds. It might not be kept in an iron vessel, which it would burst, but had to be wrapped in a woollen cloth and placed in a basket, lead-lined and filled with barleycorn. After the destruction of the temple, the shamir vanished. The Hoopoe also carried the letter from Solomon to the Queen of Sheba, inviting her to visit him.

It is an unmistakable bird, with a large erectile crest and the tongue-twisting zoological name of *Upupa epops*. It breeds in the warmer, northern parts of the Bible lands and overwinters in tropical Africa. It is listed today as a common resident.

H ORNET

Hornet (*Vespa crabro*)
(Photograph: Sam
Beaufoy)

'And I will send hornets
before thee which shall
drive out the Hivite, the
Canaanite and the Hittite
from before thee.'
(Exodus 23:28)

Mentioned three times, and on each occasion as an instrument of punishment of God: 'I will send hornets before thee which shall drive out the Hivite, the Canaanite and the Hittite from before thee' (Exod 23:28), and 'Moreover the Lord thy God will send the hornet among them until they that are left, and hide themselves from thee, shall be destroyed' (Deut 7:20), and 'I sent the hornet before you which drave them out before you' (Joshua 24:12).

The Hebrew word is *Zira* and there is no need for a dispute as to its translation, although it should be mentioned that some scholars have thought it to be simply a figure of speech and that the hornets were simply an image for the terrors that God inspired in His enemies, just as the Latin *oestrus*, a gadfly, is used for the frenzy which that insect can cause. There is no reason to suppose that God would not use natural means to affect His purpose, however, and so there is every reason to accept that the word *Zira* means *Vespa orientalis*, the Oriental Wasp.

Hebrew lore has it that the hornets destroyed the army of the Amorites: two hornets pursued each soldier, one biting each eye and then their poison finally killing those blinded by having been bitten. They remained, however, on the east side of the Jordan river and did not follow the Israelites across, but congregated on the river bank and spat their venom across at the Canaanites, who were blinded by it. Wasps were included among the natural plagues from which God was asked for deliverance by the Hebrews, and their extermination on the Sabbath was one of the few activities allowed.

There were four species of hornet in Bible lands, two of which constructed their nests of *papier mâché* in trees and bushes and two underground or in cavities among the rocks. They are still capable of causing stampedes among cattle or horses if their nests are disturbed.

HORSE

There are 149 references to the horse, using mainly the Hebrew words *Sus* and *Paras* and the Greek *Hippos*. There is no dispute about the translation, but there is an important fact for us to grasp when we read the word today: the horse is always connected with kings, with warriors, or with war. We never find it in the most familiar contexts of our own age: those of sport or of agriculture. And so, when we hear Christ's mission heralded in Zech 9:9 'riding upon an ass', we miss the point of the entry into Jerusalem if we forget the place of the horse in the society of the time (see ASS).

The Israelites would have been familiar with the horse in Egypt (Gen 47:17), but they were forbidden by God to procure them for themselves (Deut 17:16). The reason is given in Isaiah 31:1-3, that, if they had a well-trained and invincible cavalry to protect them they would withdraw their trust in God as their saviour, would have become like the surrounding idolatrous nations, and have lost their special relationship with God. By the time of Solomon, however, a cavalry force had been established and horses were imported from Egypt and Assyria (1 Kings 4:26; 10:26-8; 2 Chron 1:14-17). The whole region around had been famous for its warhorses from the earliest times, and the prophets always tell of the invaders having horses and chariots (Jer 47:3; 50:42; Ezek 26:7; 38:4).

The horse was a symbol of strength and swiftness which excited admiration and awe, the prophets complaining some-times that it was more highly regarded by politicians than the God of Israel (Isaiah 30:15-16); and 'Some trust in chariots and some in horses, but we will remember the name of the Lord

Grey Arab Stallion
(*Equus* sp.)

'He saith among the trumpets Ha, Ha; and he smelleth the battle afar off . . . (Job 39:25)

our God' (Psa 20:7). The most magnificent picture of the warhorse as seen by the Israelites is that in Job 39:

> . . . the glory of his nostrils is terrible. He paweth in the valley and rejoiceth in his strength: he goeth on to meet the armed men . . . He swalloweth the ground with fierceness and rage . . . He saith among the trumpets Ha, ha; and he smelleth the battle afar off, the thunder of the captains, and the shouting.

Although there is little evidence that the Semites ever worshipped the horse, they may well have been influenced by the introduced cults from surrounding lands where horses and chariots were worshipped by idolatrous kings and dedicated to the sun (2 Kings 23:11). Horses were sacrificed to the sun at Mount Taletum and annually thrown into the sea at Rhodes. There is a tale in Hebrew lore which illustrates the special significance of the horse: when God decided to install Enoch as king over all the angels in heaven, he sent down a horse to collect him and, after journeying on the horse for six days, Enoch was taken up to heaven in a fiery chariot drawn by fiery chargers. In Egypt, slaves were not permitted to ride horses, and Nebuchadnezzar entered the Holy of Holies riding one.

So the horse in the Bible is almost entirely used as a metaphor for that which is swift and strong, magnificent and warlike, and the trappings of earthly splendour.

H ORSELEACH

Used only once, in a rather puzzling context: 'The horseleach hath two daughters, crying, Give, give' (Prov 30:15). The Hebrew word is *Aluka*, identified by modern zoologists as *Hirudinia* which are leeches. None of the modern translations manages to clarify this rather obscure passage, but they simply substitute 'leech' for the AV 'horseleach'. The meaning seems to be that leeches are never sated with blood, but cry always for more. The word 'horse leech' was well known in AV times. It signified a large aquatic sucking worm (*Haemopsis sanguisuga*) which, by the mid-sixteenth century was used figuratively of a rapacious or insatiable person. Pistol, in *Henry V*, uses the term in his rallying cry:

Let us to France, like horse leeches, my boys.
To suck, to suck, the very blood to suck!
(*Henry V*, Act 2, Scene 3)

Leeches are external parasites that occur on land, in the sea, or in fresh water. They range in size from about half an inch (*Glossiphonia heteroclita*) to about eight inches for the medicinal leech (*Hirudo medicinalis*), the most familiar to us, if only by reputation. They are common in Bible lands and Canon Tristram records that his horses suffered a great deal from attacks by leeches which would breed in the stagnant

Leech (*Hirudo medicinalis*)

'The horseleach hath two daughters crying Give, give . . .' (Proverbs 30:15)

waters and then attach themselves to the nostrils or palates of the animals while drinking. It seems that today, because of the drainage of swamps and the tapping of small rivers, the population of leeches has been much reduced, but they are taking up new habitats in the recently founded fish farms.

H YENA

The word is not found in the AV, but the context in which some modern translations have placed it seems a strong possibility: 'And the wild beasts of the islands shall cry in their desolate houses' (Isaiah 13:22).

The Hebrew word is *Zevoa*, which means literally 'howling creature', and the RV reads 'and wolves shall cry in their castles'. Modern translators seem to prefer Wolves and Jackals here, though the NIV has, with pleasing alliteration, 'Hyenas shall howl in her strongholds'. There is an important clue to the meaning in the name of the Valley of Zeboim, mentioned in 1 Samuel 13:18, which is still called by the Arabs the Valley of the Hyena (*Shukh el Dubba*), so it seems likely that the word Zevoa does indeed refer to the Striped Hyena (*Hyaena hyaena*), which is still common in Syria.

In Hebrew legend, the hyena was known for its habit of annually changing its sex and also for the ability to give birth through the mouth and of being capable of transforming itself into a number of different shapes, always ending up as a demon. In AV times the hyena was known to work magic, having the ability to come to houses in the night and call out of the darkness to the inhabitants in a human voice; it could even call out the hounds in the voice of their master and then attack and eat them. Pliny records that hyenas could hypnotise humans by their magic arts: 'In the hyena itself there is a certain magical virtue transporting the mind of man or woman and ravishing their senses so as that it will allure them unto her very strangely.' The hyena was very common in Bible lands, inhabiting a wide range of habitats including the deserts and the forests but more particularly the caves and tombs where Canon Tristram once found a heap of bones of Camel, oxen and sheep, including a pile of seven Camels' skulls which had

baffled even their gnawing powers. They were, next to the Jackal, the most numerous beast of prey and graveyards were often visited by groups of them at night where bodies would be dug up and eaten if the graves were not protected by a covering of heavy stones.

Today they are rarer, but the Striped Hyena is the largest of the predators, a male weighing up to 80 pounds. They inhabit mainly the Judaean desert and the Negev and are protected by law. They feed at night, either on small animals such as turtle, hedgehog or porcupine, or on carrion which they will feast on in an established order, the pregnant females being given priority. They always leave the carcase at daybreak, often tearing off a chunk of flesh just before leaving, to carry back to their lair.

Striped Hyena (*Hyaena hyaena*)

'And the wild beasts of the islands shall cry in their desolate houses...' (Isaiah 13:22)

I BEX

Nubian Ibex (*Capra ibex nubiana*)

'The high hills are a refuge for the wild goats.' (Psalm 104:18)

This word is not in the AV but modern translators and zoologists agree that it is the correct translation of the Hebrew *Ye'elim*, for which the AV has 'wild goat'. The Ibex (*Capra ibex nubiana*) is closely related to the goat and looks very like one with its sturdy body, strong legs and goat-like beard in the male. The adult stands about 85 cm at the shoulder and has magnificent horns sweeping high and wide over its back, the male's reaching up to 125 cm. The female's horns are shorter and more slender. It lives among the rocks on the mountain slopes and its flexible hooves enable it to get a purchase on the smallest protuberances so that whole herds of Ibex have been reported as scaling apparently vertical rock faces. They are also very agile jumpers and can leap astonishing distances both vertically and horizontally if startled.

For most of the year they live in segregated herds, the males and females congregating and feeding separately. In the autumn, at the time of the rutting season, they come together for mating and then the following spring, usually around the end of March, the pregnant females break away and give birth to one or two young which, after a week or so, are ready to rejoin the herd with their mothers. Then the females with their young and the adolescent males go off in one direction and the mature males in another until the autumn reunion.

Because the Ibex was long considered to have special therapeutic qualities – every part of its body was good for something and it has been described as a walking chemist's shop – they were extensively hunted and this beautiful animal, which once ranged from the Syrian mountains down to the Sudan and Eritrea, is now a protected species living among the rocks of En Gedi, where David fled to seek refuge from Saul.

JACKAL

Not found in the AV, though from the RV onwards translations have so rendered the three Hebrew words *Iyim*, literally 'howlers' for which AV has 'wild beasts', *Tan*, for which AV has 'dragon', and *Shu'al* for which AV has 'fox'.

There is a general consensus today that, in the passages quoted below, 'jackal' is the correct translation and the

Golden Jackal (*Canis aureus*)

'I will make the towns of Judah desolate, a haunt of jackals.' (Jeremiah 10:22)

quotations are taken from NIV. The principle context of this animal is one of destruction and desolation as when the wrath of the Lord is visited on Babylon and 'desert creatures will lie there, jackals will fill her houses' (Isaiah 13:22). Edom, it is written, will become 'a haunt for jackals, a home for wolves' (Isaiah 34:13). The phrase is frequently repeated in the threats to other doomed cities: 'I will make Jerusalem a heap of ruins, a haunt of jackals' (Jer 9:11); 'I will make the towns of Judah desolate, a haunt of jackals' (Jer 10:22); 'Hazor will become a haunt of jackals, a desolate place forever' (Jer 49:33); 'Mount Zion will lie desolate with jackals prowling over it' (Lam 3:18). And when the authors wish to depict the extremes of human misery, the jackal is again called on: 'I have become a brother of jackals, a companion of owls' (Job 30:29) and 'I will go about barefoot and naked, I will howl like a jackal' (Micah 1:8). On the last days, the land of the redeemed is contrasted with the former desolation of the habitation of the jackals: 'In the haunts where jackals once lay, grass and reeds and papyrus will grow' (Isaiah 36:7).

In all of these contexts the word 'dragon' would fit equally well; and it may be the desire of the modern translators to purge the Bible of what they regard as superstitious connotations that has led to the substitution of the Jackal. On the other hand, the Jackal is still, and has been for centuries, the most common four-footed predator of Bible lands and must have been very familiar to the Bible writers. It would be strange were it to be omitted from the scriptures. This animal, also known as the Oriental or Golden Jackal (*Canis aureus*), is very similar in appearance to the fox, having a slightly lighter coat and being most readily distinguished from the fox by its habit of hunting in packs rather than as an individual. This has led many commentators to substitute 'Jackal' for 'fox' in the well-known story which tells of Samson's catching 300 foxes and, having tied firebrands to their tails, releasing them to run through the corn of the Philistines. He would never, it is claimed, have managed to catch 300 foxes, which go abroad singly, but might more easily have secured 300 Jackals, which go about in packs. We do not attempt to reduce the other feats of Samson to what we find more easily credible in our own time and there seems no good reason to do so with this one.

In Jewish legend, the Jackal is said to hate its young, and even the nursing mothers would devour their offspring as they suckle, were it not that God veils their faces so that she cannot see them.

Jackals seem to be successful and prolific, giving birth to between three and eight young, after a gestation period of 60 to 63 days, once a year, and becoming sexually mature at around twelve months of age. They are reduced in number today, partly by hunting and partly by the improved hygiene of the country which reduces the available carrion. But their long, haunting, and penetrating call can still be heard around the towns and villages of the Bible lands at night.

KITE

Only found in the list of unclean birds: 'And there are they which ye shall have in abomination ... and the vulture, and the kite after his kind' (Lev 11:13-14 and Deut 14:13).

The Hebrew word is *Aia* and the translation has caused some dispute: the RV has 'falcon' and the RSV has 'buzzard'. Modern translators prefer kite or falcon. The answer seems to be that there are two words in Hebrew which mean 'kite': *Aia* and *Daia*. We know that the latter is cognate with an Arabic

Black Kites (*Milvus migrans*)

'And these are they which ye shall have in abomination . . . the vulture and the kite after his kind.' (Leviticus 11:13-14)

word '*H'Daya*', which means 'Black Kite'. There are two species of kite in Bible lands, the Red and the Black. So it is reasonable to suppose that '*Aia*' means 'Red Kite'.

The kite has long had a reputation as a scavenger and would be well known to the AV translators in that role. When Hamlet screams out his frustrations at the unpunished villainy of Claudius he cries 'I should have fatted all the region kites with this slave's offal' (Act 2 Scene 2) and Autolycus, in *The Winter's Tale*, says 'When the kite builds, look to lesser linen' (Act 4 Scene 2). This habit of stealing lesser linen was recorded by Canon Tristram who speaks of the kite as having a nest which is 'the marine storeshop of the desert . . . decorated with whatever scraps of bournouses [hoods worn by Arabs] and coloured rags as can be collected'. The Black Kite is *Milvus migrans*; it is shaped rather like a buzzard, with broad, rounded wings and a shallow forked tail not easily seen in flight. It is dark brown in colour and is one of the world's most abundant birds of prey, hunting gregariously and frequently over or near water. It eats almost any kind of animal matter and lives alongside man, performing a useful function as a scavenger – sufficient reason for it to be declared unclean. It is listed today as a common winter visitor. The Red Kite (*Milvus milvus*), which is much rarer, is rather larger, with a whitish head and underparts of a pale reddish chestnut colour. It is today mostly confined to woodland areas, and is listed as a very rare winter visitor.

LAPWING

A list word, found only in the unclean birds: 'And these are they which ye shall have in abomination . . . and the lapwing and the bat' (Lev 11:13-19 and Deut 14:18). The Hebrew word is *Dukipat* and only the AV so translates it. Other versions have HOOPOE (q.v.).

But there would have been little surprise for the AV translators to find the Lapwing classed as an abomination: legend had it that this bird mocked at Christ on the cross and was condemned to wander the wilds crying mournfully till the end of time. The naturalist Bartholomew recorded that 'The Lapwing eateth man's dirt; for it is a bird most filthy and unclean, and it is copped [that is, crested] on the head and dwelleth always in graves or dirt. And if a man anoint himself with her blood before he goeth to sleep, he shall see fiends busy to strangle and snare him.'

The Lapwing (*Vanellus vanellus*) is the commonest of the plovers and is easily recognised by its bright black and white colours, its broad and rounded wings and its crest. Its call has given it the vernacular name of 'Peewit' and the loud lapping sound of its wings, particularly in its display flight, gave it its common name. It is very gregarious, huge flocks being frequently seen on farmlands, marshy fields and along mud flats and estuaries. It is listed today as a common winter visitor.

Lapwing (*Vanellus vanellus*)

L EOPARD

There are seven references in the Old Testament and one in the New Testament. The Hebrew word is *Namer*, which is cognate with the Arabic *Nimr*, found in place names such as Nimrah (Num 32:3) and Bethelnimrah (Num 32:36), and 'the waters of Nimrim' (Isaiah 15:6). The Greek word is *Pardalis*. The habit of including the Leopard as part of a place name is instanced in the Song of Solomon: 'Come with me from Lebanon, my spouse ... from the lions' dens, from the mountains of the leopards' (S. of S. 4:8). From its practice of lying long in silent waiting, usually stretched close along the branch of a tree to spring down on its prey comes the reference in the prophets: 'as a leopard by the way will I observe them' (Hos 13:7) and 'a wolf of the evenings shall spoil them, a leopard shall watch over their cities' (Jer 5:6). The savage nature of the leopard is unchanging, as recorded in the proverb still in current use: 'Can the Ethiopian change his skin or the leopard his spots?' (Jer 13:23). But, in the last days, when the peaceable kingdom shall be established, Isaiah prophesies that the Leopard will, indeed, change his spots: 'The wolf also shall dwell with the lamb, and the leopard shall lie down with the kid' (Isaiah 11:6). The prophesy of the Macedonian or Persian Empire is likened to a winged leopard: 'After this I beheld, and lo, another, like a leopard, which had upon the back of it the four wings of a fowl' (Dan 7:6) and the New Testament prophesy of Revelations also has 'the beast which I saw was like unto a leopard' (Rev 13:2).

In all of these references there is general agreement that the animal referred to is the true Leopard, *Panthera pardus*. Only in the text from Habakkuk, 'Their horses also are swifter than the leopard' (Hab 1:8) is there some doubt, modern commentators pointing out that the most probable animal here is the Cheetah (*Acinonyx jubatus*), which is particularly noted for its speed and is easily confused with the Leopard, the chief difference being that its skin is marked with rosettes as distinct from the solid spots of the Leopard. The Cheetah is often called the 'hunting leopard' and was trained for the chase, so this interpretation may well be correct.

In Hebrew lore, the Leopard was noted for its strength and ferocity. The dying Judah, boasting of the gifts which the Lord had bestowed on him, told how he had seized a Leopard which

had attacked his dog at Hebron, and flung it by the tail down to the coast; enemies were to be crushed 'as a leopard crunches the skull of a kid'; and, on the steps of the throne of Solomon, were golden leopards which, by the operation of machinery, would growl at the approach of a visitor.

Leopard (*Panther pardus*)

'A wolf of the evening shall spoil them, a leopard shall watch over their cities.' (Jeremiah 5:6)

There was some confusion in AV times as to the distinction between the Leopard, the Pard, and the Panther. An Arabic legend had it that some men had been of good disposition, but had washed themselves in milk and so turned into Panthers, the enemies of mankind. And the naturalist Bartholomew thought that Leopards were the offspring of a Panther with a Lioness. Topsell, in his *Four-footed Beasts*, tried to clear the matter up but only confused it more:

The Panther is the female and the Pard the male. When the Lion covereth the Pard, then is the whelp called the Leopard,

95

or Libbard; but when the Pard covereth the Lioness, then it is called a Panther. The only difference between the Leopard, the Pard and the Lion is that the Leopard, or Pard, have no manes ... And, truly, in my opinion, they are all one kind of beast and differ in quality only through adulterous generation.

Things are clearer today: the genus *Panthera* includes all the big cats, Lion, Tiger, and Leopard, for which Panther is just another name. The Cheetah is a cat apart, differing from the others in having non-retractile claws. Leopards, not being highly specialised in habitat, were widespread in Bible lands, from the mountains to the desert plains, but have been heavily hunted and are now found only occasionally in the Judaean wilderness or the forests of Galilee.

LEVIATHAN

There are four references, all in the Old Testament, which all present this animal as being huge, terrifying and invincible, except by the might of the Lord. God taunts Job with his impotence: 'Canst thou draw out leviathan with an hook? or his tongue with a cord which thou lettest down?' (Job 41:1); 'In that day the Lord with his sore and great and strong sword shall punish leviathan the piercing serpent, even leviathan that crooked serpent; and he shall slay the dragon that is in the sea' (Isaiah 27:1). The psalmist exults in the might of the Lord: 'Thou breakest the heads of leviathan in pieces, and gavest him to be meat to the people inhabiting the wilderness' (Psa 74:14), a reference to an ancient Hebrew legend, of which more below; and, in thanking God for his great works, the psalmist sings 'O Lord ... the earth is full of thy riches ... so is this great and wide sea ... There go the ships: there is that leviathan whom thou hast made to play therein' (Psa 104: 24-6).

It seems clear that a mythical animal is intended here, though there have been interpretations of naturalists which connect Leviathan with an animal which inhabits the Bible lands today. In Hebrew lore, Leviathan is an ancient myth, and

Leviathan

'O Lord the earth is full of thy riches . . . so is this great and wide sea . . . There go the ships: there is that Leviathan whom thou hast made to play therein.' (Psalm 104:24-6)

modern scholars have connected it with the Babylonian creation myths. He was created ruler over all the sea animals on the fifth day of creation. Originally, God created a pair of them but realising that their united strength might annihilate the earth, God killed the female. Leviathan is so enormous that, to quench his thirst, he needs all the waters of the Jordan; when he is hungry, his hot breath makes the waters of the sea boil; the only creature that can control him is the stickleback, a tiny fish, specially created by God for that purpose, and of which he stands in great awe. The fins of Leviathan are so brilliant that the sun is dimmed by their radiant light; and his eyes shine so brightly that they light up the sea. Leviathan is a creature of such magnificence, strength and beauty that he is the fitting plaything of God at the end of each day. For three hours God reads the Torah, then for three hours he judges the world; for the third three hours he attends to the needs of all living creatures, and for the last three hours he sports with Leviathan. In the last days, Leviathan will be slain and God will make tents of his skin to shelter the pious while they feast on his flesh. Then, what is left of his skin will be stretched as a glorious canopy over Jerusalem and the radiance from it will illuminate the whole world.

So much for the myth. Naturalists have found in the description of Leviathan in Job 41 much to connect it with the crocodile; the tough skin, the armoured back which cannot be pierced by iron nor fish hook, and the consequences of once securing the beast when 'he maketh the deep to boil like a pot' (v. 31).

The crocodile was common in Egypt in Bible times, when it was worshipped as the emblem of the Pharaoh and venerated as the symbol of the sun. In the Zerka river, which flows down to the Mediterranean from the hills of Samaria, crocodiles were mentioned by Pliny and Strabo and seen a thousand years later by Crusaders. The Nile Crocodile (*Crocodylus niloticus*), which is by far the most common of the four species found in Africa, grows to around 13 feet in length and lives in and on the banks of rivers, the placing of its eyes and nostrils high on its head enabling it to see and breath whilst lying so covered by water or mud as to be almost invisible. The female makes a nest on the banks of a river, where she lays her eggs and watches over them until they are hatched by the heat of the sun. Crocodiles have been so intensively hunted because of the high prices paid for their skins that they are no longer found in the wild in Bible lands.

LICE

They occur only in the context of the plague visited on the land of Egypt and recorded in Exodus:

> Stretch out thy rod and smite the dust of the land that it may become lice throughout all the land of Egypt ... and they did so and it became lice in man and in beast; all the dust of the land became lice through all the land of Egypt. And the magicians did so with their enchantments to bring forth lice but they could not: so there were lice upon man and upon beast. (Exod 8:16-18)

And the plague is recalled by the psalmist: 'He spake and there came divers sorts of flies and lice in all their coats' (Psa 105:31).

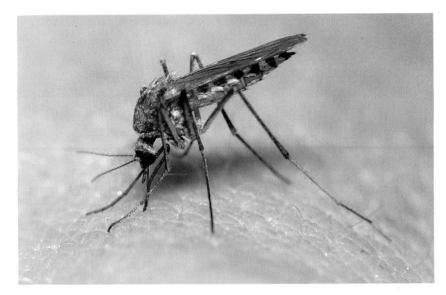

Mosquito biting
(*Culex* sp.) (Photograph:
Larry West)

'All the dust of the land
became lice through all
the land of Egypt.'
(Exodus 8:17)

The Hebrew word is *Chinnim* and there seems to be no reason to abandon the AV translation, though some of the modern versions have substituted 'maggots' (NEB), 'mosquitoes' (JB) or 'gnats' (NAS, GNB, NIV). The point, according to Hebrew lore, was that the third plague was beyond the power of the magicians to imitate because the demons who helped them could only produce objects of the size of a barley grain or larger. So the lice defeated them.

Lice would be particularly telling, so Canon Tristram pointed out, because the Egyptians were particularly horrified by vermin: their priests shaved their heads every third day so that they could not harbour lice and so be polluted when performing religious rites. So the plague of lice was not only a noisome visitation on them but a means of polluting them. Modern zoologists have translated *Chinnim* as the Human louse (*Pediculus humanus*).

These were, of course, familiars of the AV translators, whose naturalists held that like many other parasites, lice were the natural products of their hosts. Bartholomew wrote: 'A Louse is a worm of the skin and grieveth more in the skin with the feet with creeping than he doth with biting and is gendered of right corrupt airs and vapours that sweat out between the skin and the flesh by pores . . . And the leaner that a louse is, the sharper she biteth.'

Lice are tiny insects that live ectoparasitically – that is, on the outside of birds and animals. They have developed over the centuries so intimately with their particular hosts that the claws of some species have formed into shapes so closely adapted to gripping the hairs that they cannot easily grip hairs of another diameter on another host. Some even confine themselves to particular areas of the body: there is a subspecies *Pediculus humanus capitis* which stays on the human head as distinct from *Pediculus humanus humanus*, the body louse. Lice are so specialised, in fact, that they have helped in the identification of the relationships between groups of birds. For example, the flamingoes would seem to be far more closely related to storks than to ducks, but their lice have helped establish that they are closer to the ducks. There are biting lice and sucking lice, the former having well developed jaws with which they scrape the skin, and the latter having highly specialised mouth parts with a toothed proboscis and three stylets which can pierce the skin and form a channel up which the blood flows.

LION

There is no problem of identification here: it is hard to mistake a Lion for anything else, though the 156 references make use of a number of different Hebrew words such as *Aryeh*, the general term for 'lion', *Cepheer*, usually a 'young lion', *Labi*, usually 'an old lion' and *Laish*, a poetic term for a lion in full strength.

The Lion was so much a part of the mythology and folklore of Bible times that almost all the contexts in which it is mentioned are metaphorical: they were familiar from common figures of speech rather than intimate field studies. So most of the references are to human qualities that are felt to be 'lion-like' rather than to the animals themselves in their natural habitat. So we have the proverb, still in use, that it is better to be a living dog than a dead Lion (Eccl 9:4), the rhetorical question 'What is stronger than a lion' (Jud 14:18) and the description of the bravest warriors as 'fearless as lions' (2 Sam 17:10).

Because the Lion was experienced, in human terms, as irresistible, it was also used as a figure for the power of evil, to be overcome only with God's help: 'the wicked ruler' is 'as dangerous as a prowling lion' (Prov 28:15); and the psalmist

cries for help because 'my soul is among lions' (Psa 57:4). On the other hand, the power and implacability of the Lion made it a fitting instrument of the wrath of God, as when the prophet of Judah, having dined out in defiance of God's command, is struck from his donkey by a Lion which then stands by the corpse and the donkey without molesting either, thus demonstrating that it acted under orders (1 Kings 30:28). And then there was the peaceloving prophet of the Syrian wars who approached his neighbour 'in the word of the Lord' and said 'Smite me!' and when the man refused to smite him, a Lion came along and slew him because he had refused the Lord's command (1 Kings 20:35-7).

These arbitrary killings are not easy to square with our notions of justice, but were related to emphasise the duty of

Lion (*Panthera leo*)

'The lion is come up from his thicket and the destroyer of the Gentiles is on his way.'
(Jeremiah 4:7)

101

God's people to obey his commands without questioning that which they could not understand. So God also sent Lions among the nations of Samaria and many were slain because they did not fear him. Because the King of Beasts was proverbially invincible, a man's status was uniquely enhanced if he managed to defeat one, and so Samson's feat in tearing a young lion apart with his bare hands sets him apart from mankind (Jud 14:5-7). And David, when trying to persuade the king that he was valiant enough to be allowed his chance at Goliath, mentions that he had killed both a Lion and a bear that came after his father's sheep (1 Sam 17:35).

There is little in any of these references to suggest that any of the authors had even seen a Lion. Their culture was shot through with the myths of Egypt and Babylon, both of which celebrated the regal majesty of Lions: the stone Lion of Babylon still stands mute witness to the awe in which the most powerful of the beasts of the field was held there; and the Egyptian goddesses Tefnut and Sekhmet were both Lionesses. The images of Lions are still found by archaeologists in Bible lands, on the stone friezes of buildings and on the brass hilts of daggers. Lions decorated the bronze tank of Solomon's palace (1 Kings 7:29) and stood, in pairs, on the six steps that led to his golden throne (1 Kings 10:20). The faces of Lions occupied an even more exalted position: they were seen by the prophet Ezekiel in his vision of the throne of God (Ezek 1:10).

But there are just two Old Testament references that seem redolent of actual experience of Lions. The first is the vivid picture called up by Isaiah to emphasise that God will not be deflected from his purpose in protecting Mount Zion: 'Like as a lion, or a young lion, roaring on his prey, when a multitude of shepherds is called forth against him, he will not be afraid of their voice, nor abase himself for the noise of them' (Isaiah 31:4). Here we can easily conjure up the picture of the shepherds joining together in shouting at a Lion which threatens their flocks – and being ignored by the beast. The second reference is from the prophet Amos who was a shepherd and who must have had the experience that prompted the lines: 'As a shepherd taketh out of the mouth of a lion two legs or a piece of an ear . . .' (Amos 3:12).

The New Testament has no new images of Lions and they are completely absent from the Gospels and Acts. The Lion of Judah occurs again in Revelations (5:5) and St Peter describes the devil as going about like a roaring Lion looking for someone to devour (1 Peter 5:8); but both are drawn from culture rather than natural observation: a Lion that roared as it went about its hunting would go hungry.

In Hebrew legend, the Lion suffered a fever all the time it was in the Ark and did not enjoy the dry food that was provided for it. But when Noah, one day, forgot to feed the Lion, the beast struck him so violently that Noah was lame for ever after and, because of this deformity, was not allowed to exercise the office of priest. The Pharoah's palace, in Egypt, was guarded by live Lions so that when Moses and Aaron visited it they had to wait at the entrance until the Lion keeper came to take them away.

Lions were prevalent in Bible lands and so must have been part of the personal experience of the people in their daily lives as well as forming part of their folklore. They were gradually destroyed by firearms and, although mentioned by the Crusaders, were extinct in the wild over a century ago.

LIZARD

Only found in the list of unclean animals: 'There also shall be unclean unto you among the creeping things that creep upon the earth ... the lizard and the snail and the mole' (Lev 11: 29-30).

The Hebrew word *Letaa* is also found in the Talmud for the *Lacertid* family of lizards and modern zoologists so identify this creature. The lizard was felt, in Hebrew folklore, to have powerfully magical properties: it was an antidote to the scorpion (also in AV folklore, see below) and could even terrify Leviathan. It has a strange relationship with other animals, as reported by an ancient Rabbi who once saw a Lion, a lizard, and a dog together. The Lion wanted to attack the dog, but dared not for fear of the lizard, which is the protector of the Lion, as the dog is the protector of the lizard.

The naturalist Bartholomew reported:

The lizard is a little beast painted on the back with shining specks, as it were stars. The lizard is so contrary to scorpions that the scorpions dread and lose comfort when they see the lizard. The lizard liveth mostly by dew; and, though he be a fair beast and fair painted, yet he is right venomous; for the

Ornate Dabb Lizard
(*Uromastrix ornatus*)

worst medicine is made of the lizard ... And the gall of the lizard stamped in water assembleth together weasels. And the lizard lurketh in winter in dens and chines, and his sight dimmeth; and in springing time he cometh out of his den, and feeleth that his sight faileth, and changeth his place, and seeketh a place toward the east, and openeth continually his eyes toward the rising of the sun until the humour in the eye be full dried and the mist wasted that is the cause of dimness in the eye.

And the lizard was, for Albertus Magnus, one of the Wonders of the World:

Take a lizard, and cut off its tail, and take what comes out because it is like quicksilver. Then take a taper, and moisten it with oil, and put it in a new lamp, and light it. That man's house will appear splendid and white or silvered.

The lizards of Bible lands vary from the tiny gecko (q.v.) to the Desert Monitor (*Varanus griseus*) which looks like a small crocodile and can grow up to four feet long.

LOCUST

By far the most important insect in the Bible. There are nine Hebrew words for it, and the one in Greek, and, in its different form, 56 references. It was in two respects an insect unique in Bible lands: it was the only one that was expressly permitted as food (Lev 11:22) and it was the only one that could lay waste the land and even blot out the sun in its migrations. So it is used in the Bible mainly as an agent of destruction, the most striking description of which is in the Book of Joel:

> For a nation is come upon my land, strong and without number, whose teeth are the teeth of a lion ... The field is wasted, the land mourneth ... Like the noise of chariots on the tops of mountains shall they leap, like the noise of a flame of fire that devoureth the stubble ... The earth shall quake before them; the heavens shall tremble; the sun and the moon shall be dark, and the stars shall withdraw their shining. (Joel 1:6-10 and 2:5-10)

Locusts constituted the eighth plague that was visited on Egypt (Exod, Chapter 10), coming out of a clear sky, the great swarms could darken the sun (Exod 10:15), and their

Locust (*Locust migratoria*)

'For a nation is come upon my land, strong and without number, whose teeth are the teeth of a lion ...' (Joel 1:6)

depredations made them a fitting image for swarming hordes (Judges 6:5; 7:12; Jer 46:23; Judith 2:20). Because they band together, they are classed by the writer of proverbs as among the little things upon the earth that are wise (Prov 30:27) and yet because they are threatening they are compared to warhorses (Joel 2:4; Revelations 9:7).

They are still eaten, after being fried in clarified butter, the legs and heads having been removed, or they can be dried and pounded into a kind of flour. They were the food of John the Baptist (Matt 3:4). There has been much argument among scholars as to the meaning of the different Hebrew words used for Locust, but a modern scholar and naturalist[1] has summed up the evidence in a series of names given for each of the stages of development of the insect. So, *arbeh* is the word used for the mature insect which has wings and a yellow-brown body. After fertilisation, the female lays her eggs in a hole in the ground and these develop into ant-like larvae called *yelek*, which are able to eat only the soft, green, shoots. Then these develop, after shedding their skins, into larger insects of a pinkish hue that are able to eat large quantities of herbage, and these are called *hasil*. It is at this stage that most of the damage to crops is done. Then the insect develops short wings and becomes a *gazam*, which attacks the bark of trees and finally, as the wings grow to their full extent, it becomes a mature *arbeh* and is ready to migrate and to reproduce itself.

It is interesting that the confusion that seems to exist in the modern versions of the Bible between the translation 'locust' and 'grasshopper', dates back to AV times, when William Harrison, writing in the Preface to Holinshed's *Chronicle* says: 'The Locust is none other creature than the grasshopper. In Barbary . . . they are eaten; nevertheless they shorten the life of the eaters by the production, at the last, of a loathsome and filthy disease.'

Both Locusts and grasshoppers belong to the family Acrididae, the grasshoppers being the familiar short green insects that sing from the meadows on sunny afternoons by rubbing their legs against the edges of their wings, the most familiar and abundant of these being the Meadow Grasshopper (*Chorthippus parallelus*); the Locust (*Schistocerca gregaria*) is larger, stronger, and capable of longer sustained flight. They are also characterised by the great invasions of cultivated areas and the devastation they can wreak. The last in the Bible lands was in 1915.

1. Yehuda Feliks in *Nature and Man in the Bible*, pp. 159-61.

MOLE

Palestine Mole Rate
(*Spalax ehrenbergi*)

There are two references, the first to the unclean list: 'These shall be unclean unto you among the creeping things that creep upon the earth ... the lizard and the snail and the mole' (Lev 11:29-30). Here the Hebrew word is *Tinshemet*, which modern zoologists prefer to translate as a monitor lizard, on the ground that the mole is practically immobile when it comes to the surface and so cannot properly be described as a 'creeping thing that creeps upon the ground'. The modern translations follow this. The second reference is to the devastation of the last days: 'In that day a man shall cast his idols of silver and his idols of gold ... to the moles and to the bats' (Isaiah 2:20). Here the Hebrew word is *Chephor-peroth*, which indicates a burrowing animal, and the modern zoologists are divided between mole and mole-rat.

Surprisingly, for it is widespread in neighbouring countries, the mole is not found in Bible lands and its ecological niche has been taken up by the Mole Rat (*Spalax ehrenbergi*), a very similar creature with eyes covered by skin and no external ears. It lives underground, making, like the mole, an extensive burrowing system with storage chambers, sleeping quarters and connecting passages. Because it finds that it can easily

107

construct its burrows in ruins and heaps of old stones, it is particularly fitted, as Canon Tristram pointed out, for the role of harbinger of desolation, which it plays in Isaiah. He found them burrowing in the rubbish around the walls of Jerusalem and kept a few in earthen jars (because they instantly gnaw through wood), feeding them on onions and soaked bread. In the wild, the Mole Rat lives on roots, either those of grass and trees or, given the chance, those found in gardens such as carrots, onions and potatoes.

MOTH

Common Clothes Moth (*Tineola bisselliella*) (Photograph: Walter Jarchow)

'Thou makest his beauty to consume away, like a moth.' (Psalm 39:11)

There are seven references in the Old Testament and one very well-known context in the New Testament. The effects of moths were well known and always destructive, so they are used in the Bible as images of destruction: 'And he, as a rotten thing, consumeth as a garment that is moth-eaten' (Job 13:28); and 'Lo, they shall all wax old as a garment; the moth shall eat them up' (Isaiah 50:9). This notion is repeated in the next chapter: 'For the moth shall eat them up like a garment' (Isaiah 51:8). The wrath of the Lord is even compared to the destructiveness of the moth: 'Therefore I will be unto Ephraim as a moth and to the House of Judah as rottenness' (Hos 5:12), and the psalmist sings 'thou makest his beauty to consume away like a moth' (Psa 39:11). There is a reference in Job, 'He buildeth his house as a moth' (Job 27:18) which has given rise to some critical argument, but the meaning seems to be that the house is as frail as the larval covering which moths construct and which is easily destroyed. Also the reference in Job to 'them that dwell in houses of clay, whose foundation is in the dust, which are crushed before the moth' is also puzzling at first sight, but may well refer to the fact that bundles of clothes can be so packed with the larvae of moths that they are eaten from within and the destruction is noticed only when they are picked up and crumble into dust, 'crushed before the moth' (Job 4:19).

The destruction of clothes by the moth in Bible lands was not an occasional or incidental occurrence, but something which, given time, was bound to happen, as recorded in the words of Christ: 'Lay not up for yourselves treasures upon earth, where moth and rust doth corrupt' (Matt 6:19-20 and Luke 12:33).

The Hebrew word is *Ash* and the Greek *Ses* and there is no doubt that these words refer to insects of the family *Tineidae*, that is, the clothes moths. These were familiar to the AV translators as dwellers in, and destroyers of, garments. And it was thought that they were engendered by the process of the corruption which they caused. Cures were popular and eccentric. Mouffet wrote, in his *Theatre of Insects*:

> Moths breed in garments so much the sooner if a spider be shut in. They that sell woollen cloths used to wrap up the skin of a bird called the Kingfisher among them, or else hang one in the shop, as a thing by a secret antipathy that moths cannot endure. Garments wrapped up in a lion's skin will never have any moths.

In today's age of cheap and easily available clothing, it is easy to miss the full force of the biblical image. Fabrics, in biblical times, were hard to acquire, involving much labour in the weaving and much expense in the dyeing; they were ranked among a man's most treasured possessions, as when Jacob expressed his love for Joseph by giving him the coat of many colours. So the corruption of the moth would have caused far more distress than it does in our times and the images would be the more powerful.

The clothes moths are tiny insects, usually with a silvery sheen, and are much maligned because although we still use the phrase 'moth-eaten', moths do not, in fact, do the damage. Clothes are eaten by their larvae, which are among the few insects that can digest the keratin of hair and feathers.

MOUSE

Golden Spiny Mouse
(*Acomys russatus*)

'They that sanctify
themselves ... eating ...
abomination and the
mouse shall be
consumed together.'
(Isaiah 66:17)

There are six references, all in the Old Testament and none of them flattering. The first is to the classification of the creature as unclean: 'These also shall be unclean unto you ... the weasel and the mouse' (Lev 11:29). In Isaiah, there is a passage which narrates the judgement of the Lord on those who have lapsed from the faith and eaten forbidden flesh in which, surprisingly, the mouse is included: 'They that sanctify themselves ... in the gardens behind one tree in the midst, eating swine's flesh and the abomination, and the mouse shall be consumed together' (Isaiah 66:17). Here commentators have suggested that the jerboa (*Jaculus orientalis*), a larger species of dormouse (*Gliridae*), or the Golden Hamster (*Mesocricetus auratus*) is the animal referred to since both are eaten in Bible lands, but the exact classification is impossible. The remaining four references are all in the story contained in the sixth chapter of 1 Samuel, in which the mice which plagued the Philistines are brought as a trespass offering, set in gold. These 'mice that mar the land' have been widely accepted by modern translators as meaning rats (NEB, NIV, JB and RAV all have 'rats', whereas GNB, AV and NAS have kept 'mice'). The reason for this proposed change is that the historian Josephus described the plague which afflicted the Philistines as a sore distemper, bringing dysentery or flux, with sudden death, which seem symptomatic of the bubonic plague transmitted by fleas that live on rats. But it seems more likely that 'the mice that mar the land' afflicted damage on the standing crops and for this, the Striped Field Mouse (*Apodemus sylvaticus*), which can suddenly explode in population density and strip fields of corn, is the most likely candidate. It is quite possible that such an explosion took place during the wars with the Philistines, as there is a well-known account in Herodotus of the mice which attacked the bow strings and leather harness of the army of Sennacherib and so made it impossible for him to continue his assault on Egypt. The Egyptians presented a golden effigy of a mouse to their gods in thanksgiving for their deliverance.

The Hebrew word is *Ahbar* and it is likely that the Hebrews tended to classify all small brown furry creatures – voles, shrews, field-mice, dormice – as 'mice' very much as we do today. The word literally means 'corn eater'. In Hebrew legend, there is a story which accounts for the shape of the mouth of the mouse. It is said that, one day on the Ark, a mouse was pursued by a cat and fled into a hole. The cat reached inside with its paw and the mouse bit it, but the cat's claw tore a hole in the mouse's cheek, widening its mouth. When the cat went away, the mouse asked Noah to sew up its cheek, which he did, using a hair from the tail of the swine. And that is why there is today a seam-like line at the corners of the mouth of the mouse.

The mouse did not have a good image in AV times, Shakespeare using it chiefly as a sign of cowardice, and the naturalist Bartholomew reported that they were able to carry off such great loads of corn at harvest time because they would lie on their backs and be loaded up with corn on their bellies and then were pulled, like sledges, by their tails to their dens. He wrote:

His urine stinketh and is contagious; and his biting is venomous and his tail is venomous ... And though mice be full grievous and noyful beasts, yet they be in many things good and profitable in medicine. Mice dirt bruised with vinegar keepeth and saveth the head from falling of hair. His new skin laid all about the heel, healeth and saveth kibes and wounds.

There are very many small brown mammals found in Bible lands today, commonly called mice, which include the jerboas, the gerbils and the Mole rats as well as the field-mice and the Edible Dormouse (*Glis glis*).

MULE

Mule (*Equus* sp.)

'And Absalom rode upon a mule, and the mule went under the thick boughs of a great oak . . .' (2 Samuel 18:9)

There are 21 references, all in the Old Testament which is rather odd because the breeding of mules was forbidden by Leviticus 19:19, which banned the mating together of different kinds of animals. They are indeed absent from the early books but they appear first in 2 Samuel 13:29, as mounts for the sons of David. In the same period, Absalom rode a mule in war (2 Sam 18:9) and Solomon even rode one when he was proclaimed king (1 Kings 1:33) and received tribute in mules (1 Kings 10:25).

The mule became common as a beast of burden (2 Kings 5:17) and as a baggage animal for supplies in war (Judith 2:17). A good mule was far more valued as a pack animal because of its endurance and sure-footedness than was a pack horse. It may well have been because of the traditional ban on the breeding of mules that they were imported, for a time, from Armenia (Ezek 27:14). On the return from Babylon, 245 mules were brought along (Ezra 2:66). The mule is classified with the horse by the psalmist as wanting in understanding and therefore needing the control of bit and bridle (Psa 32:9). In Hebrew legend, Anah, the descendant of Esau, being himself the product of an incestuous union (his mother was the mother of his father, Zibeon) tried to bring about unnatural unions among animals and was the first to mix the horse with the ass to produce the mule.

There is a curious note in Pliny, where he recommends that mules be given wine 'to break them of their flinging and wincing', but the naturalist Bartholomew disagreed: 'Wine is forbidden the mule', he wrote. 'The more water that the mule drinketh, the more good his meat doth him.' Which is perfectly true. The mule could not, of course, have occurred naturally since the wild ass and the horse lead such separate lives, but the crossing of the male ass with the mare has proved to be very profitable to man because the product is, in so many ways, in the harsh conditions of Bible lands, superior to both.

NIGHT HAWK

Nightjar (*Caprimulgus europaeus*)

A list word only. 'And these are they which ye shall have in abomination among the fowls ... the owl and the night hawk' (Lev 11:13-16 and Deut 14:15). Because the Hebrew word *Tahmes* only occurs in this context, its exact meaning is not clear and most modern translations have rendered it as some species of owl. It is interesting that the word 'nighthawk' is first recorded in 1611, the date of the AV, and so possibly the translators of the AV were the first to use it. It is no longer in current use but, in dialect, can mean the nightjar or, as it is called in some areas, the 'goatsucker'. The zoological name *Caprimulgus* is from the Greek, meaning 'goatsucker', and the belief that this bird was in the habit of stealing milk from the udders of goats at night dates back to Aristotle. There is an American Nighthawk, which is of the *Caprimulgidae* family, but this is a very rare vagrant to the Old World and is unlikely to be the bird referred to.

The Nightjar proper (*Caprimulgus europaeus*), which winters in Africa, does pass through Bible lands in the summer. It is a nocturnal bird, which would give rise to suspicions that it was unclean in its habits, and spends the day lying along the branch of a tree, almost invisible because of its superb cryptic coloration of mottled brown. At night it hunts moths and beetles with its excellent vision from large eyes and darting flight. It is listed today as a common passage migrant.

OSPREY

Another list word: 'And these are they which ye shall have in abomination ... the eagle and the ossifrage and the osprey' (Lev 11:13 and Deut 14:12). The Hebrew word is *Ozniah*, which has been variously identified by modern translators as one of the eagles or vultures. There has long been some confusion as to the precise identification of these large birds of prey, Pliny having recorded that Ospreys force their young to look directly at the sun in order to improve their vision, which is a practice attributed to the eagle (q.v.) and also suggesting that Ospreys are a sort of mongrel eagle which have the habit of bringing up as their own the young which the eagles cast out of their nests. There is also a practice recorded in *Hortus*

Osprey (*Pandion haliaetus*)

'And these are they which ye shall have in abomination... the eagle and the ossifrage and the osprey.' (Leviticus 11:13)

Sanitatis, of the early sixteenth century, that 'Ospreys are called ossifragi because they drop bones from on high and break them' (see next entry).

But the true Osprey (*Pandion haliaetus*) is seen, albeit rarely, in Bible lands today and its status there is unlikely to have changed greatly down the centuries since it only occasionally overwinters along the sea coasts. Because it lives on fish, it is usually associated with water and is therefore rather easier to spot among the large birds of prey with its white head and underparts and its habit of flapping slowly, like a large and thick-set gull, or hovering high over the waves before suddenly swooping down to take a fish in its powerful talons.

OSSIFRAGE

A list word: 'And these are they which ye shall have in abomination ... the eagle and the ossifrage and the osprey' (Lev 11:13 and Deut 14:12). The Hebrew word is *Peres* and modern zoologists have identified this with the Lammergeier, or Bearded Vulture (*Gypaetus barbatus*). The word means 'breaker' and the identification is based on the Lammergeier's habit of dropping bones from a great height onto rocks in

Lammergeier (*Gypaetus barbatus*)

order to break them into small enough pieces to swallow. The name Ossifrage is from the Latin meaning 'bone-breaker'. It is in use today for both the Osprey (q.v.) and the Lammergeier.

Tristram records seeing the Lammergeiers floating singly or in pairs along the edges of ravines, and noted their habit, when coming to a corner, of keeping their distance from the cliff edge instead of cutting across. He also records that they will kill lambs, kids or even hares, by pushing them over the cliffs. It seems likely that the Lammergeier was responsible for the death of the Greek dramatist Aeschylus who, having been told by the oracle that he would be killed by a blow from heaven, expired when a passing bird dropped a tortoise on his bald head, mistaking it for a stone.

The Lammergeier is the largest vulture today in Bible lands and is classified as a resident, though rare. It can reach almost four feet from beak to tail and appears almost completely black in flight, the rufous head and neck being developed only in the mature male.

116

OSTRICH

When this bird is mentioned in Lamentations, the context simply suggests – without explanation – that it is noted for its cruelty: 'The daughter of my people is become cruel like the ostriches in the wilderness' (Lam 4:3). And the nature of the cruelty of the Ostrich, which may puzzle us today, is set out in Job 39 which tells that the Ostrich 'leaves her eggs in the earth and warmeth them in dust, and forgetteth that the foot may crush them, or that the wild beast may break them. She is hardened against her young ones, as though they were not hers ... because God hath deprived her of wisdom' (Job 39:14-17).

As to the stupidity of the Ostrich, this was held to be demonstrated by its habit of hiding its head in the sand in the belief that if it could not see, then it could not be seen by, an enemy. Pliny records that 'the veriest fools they be of all others – for as high as the rest of their body is, yet if they thrust their head and neck once into any shrub or bush and get it hidden they think they are safe enough and that no man seeth

Ostrich (*Struthio camelus*)

'The daughter of my people is become cruel like the ostriches in the wilderness.' (Lamentations 4:3)

them'. But as to the neglect of the eggs, this seems to be based simply on the observation that, as there are few hiding places in the desert, the Ostrich's 'nest' tends to be simply a shallow depression in the sand, usually scooped out by the male bird, in which the best protection of the eggs is their cryptic coloration. It could well be that the notion that the Ostrich does not care for her young arose from the bird's habit of running away from the nest on the approach of a predator. But this is a distraction technique: they will make themselves conspicuous and flap their wings to attract the attention of any animal or person who threatens, and thus lead them away from the eggs. And so here the writing seems to be based on observation, as is the next comment of Job that 'What time she lifteth up herself on high she scorneth the horse and his rider' (Job 39:18). The Ostrich can outrun all its natural enemies and its ability to outstrip the Greek cavalry was recorded with astonishment by Xenophon.

The naturalist Bartholomew adds another dimension to the scorn of the Ostrich for the horse and rider: 'The ostrich hateth the horse by kind, and is so contrary to the horse that he may not see the horse without fear. And if an horse is come against him, he raiseth up his wings as it were against his enemy and compelleth the horse to flee with beating of his wings.'

The wild Ostriches of Bible lands were a distinct subspecies (*Struthio camelus camelus*), rather smaller than their African relatives, which flourished for many centuries between the Syrian desert and Saudi Arabia, but finally became extinct when the last one was washed away in a flood in Southern Jordan in 1966. They are kept today in the Hai-Bar Biblical Wildlife Reserve, which is at Arava, in south Israel.

OWL

These are first mentioned as unclean in the list of Leviticus (11:16-17) and thereafter, in a further 15 references, as indicating darkness, desolation and ruins. They dwell in the dilapidations of Babylon when its glory has been overthrown (Isaiah 13:21) and after the judgement of the Lord has been visited on Edom, owls shall join with dragons and satyrs in

taking possession of the wasted land (Isaiah 34:13-14). Personal affliction is described by Job as being 'a brother to dragons and a companion to owls' (Job 30:29) and the psalmist laments that in his distress he is 'like an owl of the desert' (Psa 102:6). Micah cries that he will 'make a wailing like the dragons and a mourning as the owls' (Micah 1:8).

Because owls are nocturnal, move silently in the darkness, are able to make sudden, unearthly sounds from a ghostly hooting to a piercing screech and, perhaps above all because they are able to look at you with both eyes at once, unblinking above human-like cheeks, they have long had a reputation for the unearthly. Pliny recorded that owls always emerge from their holes tail first because their heads are so heavy; and Albertus Magnus wrote that, if a man put the heart of an owl under his armpit, then dogs would not bark at him. Owls were thought in AV times to inhabit graves by day and, if seen abroad in the cities during daylight hours, betokened the destruction of the place. In *Julius Caesar* we hear of the omen: 'The bird of night did sit, even at noon-day upon the market place, hooting and shrieking' (Act 1, Scene 3).

There are 13 different Hebrew words which the translators and commentators have identified as one or another species of owl. And the problem is that few of them are agreed. The AV knows only three owls: the Great, the Little and the Screech.

Hume's Tawny Owl (*Strix butleri*)

'And thorns shall come up in her palaces . . . and it shall be an habitation of dragons and a court for owls.' (Isaiah 34:13)

But modern versions have expanded this through research and speculation on biological and philological grounds to include the Short-eared (*Asio flammeus*), the Long-eared (*Asio otus*), the Tawny (*Strix aluco*), the Barn (*Tyto alba*), the Eagle (*Bubo bubo*), the Brown Fish (*Ketupa zeylonensis*), the Scops (*Otus scops*) and the Little (*Athene noctua*).

It is very improbable that the biblical authors were as precise as modern zoologists in their classifications and since owls, being nocturnal birds, are very difficult to distinguish between closely related species, the most likely way in which the authors of Old Testament times would have divided the owls is that of size: the large, the middle-sized, and the small. In other words, the threefold division of the AV. So the Eagle Owl and the Fish Owl would occupy the large class, being both around two feet tall; the Long-eared, Short-eared, Tawny and Barn Owls, are all around a foot tall and would occupy the middle division; and the Little and Scops Owls, being around eight inches, would be the small.

PALMERWORM

Locust (*Locusta migratoria*)

'Your olive trees increased, the palmerworm devoured them.' (Amos 4:9)

One of the creatures of the AV which has been lost in modern translations. The palmerworm is an instrument of God's judgement on the people who have lapsed from the faith: 'I have smitten you with blasting and mildew ... when your gardens and your vineyards ... increased, the palmerworm devoured them' (Amos 4:9) and 'that which the palmerworm hath left hath the locust eaten' (Joel 1:4); 'I will restore to you the years that the locust hath eaten ... the caterpillar and the palmerworm, my great army which I sent among you' (Joel 2:25). The Hebrew word is *Gazam* and it is generally agreed among modern translators that it represents a stage in the development of the Locust (see LOCUST). But there was a palmerworm written of in English as early as 1560; it was a hairy caterpillar of a migratory or wandering habit, destructive to vegetation. The name comes from the palmer, or pilgrim from the Holy Land who would carry, as a sign that he has completed his pilgrimage, a palm leaf to excite the admiration and envy of others. Chaucer mentions him in the prologue to his Canterbury Tales: 'And palmeres for to seeken strange strandes'.

The name palmerworm is still given in America to the larva of a tineid moth *Ypsolophus pometellus*, which feeds on the leaves of apple trees.

P ARTRIDGE

Both references to this bird are using its behaviour as an image or figure of speech, which implies that the behaviour was sufficiently well known for the image to be effective, and it therefore merits our attention today. The first reference is in the words of David: 'For the king of Israel is come out to seek a flea, as when one doth hunt a partridge in the mountains' (2 Sam 26:20). Here David is conveying the impression of running from cover to cover, like the partridge which will refuse to fly until the last moment, dashing from bush to bush until it is finally flushed out into the air.

The second reference has given rise to different interpretations. The AV has simply: 'As the partridge sitteth on eggs and hatcheth them not: so he that getteth riches and not by right shall leave them in the midst of his days' (Jer 17:11). The meaning seems to be quite clearly that the partridge sits on eggs but does not succeed in hatching them; so her efforts are as vain as the unearned riches which a man leaves when he dies in the midst of his days. But the modern translations place a different emphasis here: RSV has 'like the partridge which gathers a brood she did not hatch', and NIV has 'that hatches eggs it did not lay'; NEB 'Like a partridge which gathers into its nest eggs which it has not laid'; and GNB, characteristically, paraphrases: 'The person who gets money dishonestly is like a bird that hatches eggs it did not lay.' Here the meaning seems to be that the partridge sits on and profits by eggs she has not laid.

It is difficult to guess at the legend or field observation that might have given rise to this figure of speech. There is an Arab belief that the hen partridge lays two eggs, in two nests, and one of them is hatched by the cock, who could be said to be profiting by an egg he did not lay, and there is even a record from the naturalist Bartholomew which is relevant to the dispute:

> The Partridge ... is so guileful that the one stealeth the eggs of the other, and sitteth abroad on them; but this fraud hath no fruit, for when the birds be haught [grown], and hear the voice of their own mother, they forsake her that brooded them when they were eggs, and kept them as her own birds, and turn and follow their own mother natural.

This would certainly bear out the belief recorded in the modern translations that the partridge profits from eggs she does not lay, but that the gain does not last.

On the other hand, the AV image of a bird that lays eggs but does not manage to hatch them, is supported by the evidence of Canon Tristram, who points out that partridge nests are so easily found and the eggs considered such a delicacy that hundreds of them are taken each spring and the partridge is robbed of her chances of a brood. The final evidence in favour of the AV version, however, is that from the *Memoires of a Jewish Zoologist*, Dr Israel Ahrani, who has found as many as 30 eggs in the nest of a Desert Partridge and suggests that this is because often two hen partridges will lay close together and then one will drive off the other and attempt to sit on the whole clutch herself. Because she is too small to incubate such a large number, which, according to the habits of birds, she constantly moves around, none of the eggs reaches the

required temperature to develop the foetus to its final stage and she abandons them all before they hatch. So the AV image is supported by field observation and is a very telling one for the man who gets hold of illegal gains but then has to leave them unexploited.

The Hebrew word is *Kore*, which simply means a caller, and the most likely bird is the Desert, or Sand Partridge (*Ammoperdix heyi*), which is a small bird, intermediate in size between a quail and a partridge, still common in Bible lands and recognised by the white mark in front of both eyes. It lives, usually in pairs, on broken or stony ground in sparse vegetation. The Chukar (*Alectoris chukar*), which is larger and has the usual partridge black and white barring on the flanks, and sounds rather like a domestic hen, is also commonly found on the edges of the desert regions.

Chukar Partridge (*Alectoris chukar*)

'For the King of Israel is come out to seek a flea, as when one doth hunt a partridge in the mountains.' (1 Samuel 26:20)

P EACOCK

Peacock (*Pavo muticus*)

'... the navy of
Tharshish, bringing gold
and silver, ivory and apes
and peacocks.' (1 Kings
10:22)

Only found in the cargoes of the ships of Solomon: 'Once in
three years came the navy of Tharshish bringing gold and
silver, ivory and apes and peacocks' (1 Kings 10:22 and 2
Chron 9:21). The word is *Tuki*, which is not pure Hebrew and
led the scholars to the identification of the bird because
Tharshish has been identified with Ceylon, and the word in
Tamil for peacock is *tokei*, hence the confidence with which
this bird is identified, although Solomon was probably the first
to import them to Bible lands. The modern translators have

abandoned peacock here, preferring 'monkeys' or 'baboons', with what terrible loss to the poetry of the passage as can be felt by those who treasure the words of John Masefield:

Quinquireme of Nineveh from distant Ophir,
Rowing home to haven in sunny Palestine
With a cargo of ivory
And apes and peacocks,
Sandalwood, cedarwood and sweet white wine.

The majesty of the peacock made it a fitting inhabitant of the steps of the golden throne of Solomon, and its beauty so struck the soldiers of the Army of Alexander on their campaigns in India that its destruction was forbidden among them. The Greeks noticed, and took a moral from, the contrast between the bird's radiant appearance and its harsh and piercing voice. And, for the AV translators, the name had a special charge because the flesh of the peacock was thought to be possessed of a magical quality that kept it from corruption, and also made it impossible to cook.

There is another reference to the peacock in Job: 'Gavest thou the goodly wings unto the peacocks? or wings and feathers unto the ostrich?' (Job 39:13), but the Hebrew word here is *Rnanim*, which modern zoologists and all modern translations agree should be 'OSTRICH' (q.v.).

PELICAN

This is first mentioned on the unclean list: 'And these are they which ye shall have in abomination ... the swan, and the pelican, and the gier eagle' (Lev 11:13-18 and Deut 14:17). The Hebrew word is *Kaat*, which means to disgorge, and it would seem to be correctly translated here since the pelican is well known for its habit of disgorging food for its young. The second context is more puzzling, being an image of loneliness and desolation: 'I am like a pelican of the wilderness: I am like an owl of the desert' (Psa 102:6). Quite what a pelican might be doing in the wilderness, since it is not given to dwelling in the desert or inhabiting ruins, has puzzled the modern

White Pelican (*Pelecanus onocrotalus*)

'I am like a pelican of the wilderness . . .' (Psalm 102:6)

translators and led some of them to suggest alternatives. NIV has 'desert owl', as does NEB; GNB has 'wild bird in the desert'; and AB, quite delightfully, has 'melancholy pelican', which has to take the prize for euphony.

The pelican was known in the age of the AV as a symbol of filial impiety: King Lear bewails ''Twas this flesh begot those pelican daughters!', and this because of the belief that the young of the pelican, as they approached adolescence, would rise up and strike their parents in rebellion. The bird also symbolised Christ because it was said, after the death of its young from the bite of its traditional enemy, the serpent, to smite its own breast and give life to them again through the warmth of its life blood.

The White Pelican (*Pelecanus onocrotalus*) is a frequent migrant to the area and one of the spectacular sights of the skies in Bible lands is the great flocks of these birds travelling between their breeding grounds on the Black Sea and their winter quarters on the lakes of Uganda. The Pink-backed Pelican (*Pelecanus rufescens*) is today a very rare accidental in the region.

126

PYGARG

Only found in the list of permitted food: 'These are the beasts which ye shall eat ... the wild goat and the pygarg' (Deut 14: 4-5). The Hebrew word is *Dishon*, identified by modern zoologists as the Addax of the north Sahara. Herodotus uses the word *pygargus* for a North African antelope which has a white rump and, as Pliny also speaks of it with the same description, it seems certain that the word does indeed refer to *Addax nasomaculatus*, the Addax.

This antelope is perfectly adapted for living in the desert: it is able to eat the dryest of herbage and to go for long periods without water. It has a long-haired beige-to-grey coloured coat which turns white in the summer and reflects the glare and heat of the sun. Its wide hooves are able to travel over the soft sands without sinking in. It was much hunted as well as being raised in captivity, and is today almost extinct in many of its natural habitats, but there is a population in the Hai-Bar Reserve which is part of a global effort to save the animal from total extinction.

Addax (*Addax nasomaculatus*)

'These are the beasts which ye shall eat ... the wild goat and the pygarg.' (Deuteronomy 14:4-5)

QUAIL

Best known for being used by God as a means of feeding the Israelites in the desert: 'And it came to pass that at even the quails came up and covered the camp' (Exodus 16:13), and they were eaten with the manna. More carefully described is the incident in Numbers:

> And there went forth a wind from the Lord and brought quails from the sea and let them fall by the camp, as it were a day's journey on this side and as it were a day's journey on the other side round about the camp, and as it were two cubits high upon the face of the earth. And the people ... gathered the quails: he that gathered least gathered ten homers.
>
> (Numbers 11:31-2)

And this was celebrated by the psalmist: 'The people asked, and he brought quails, and satisfied them with the bread of heaven' (Psa 105:40). The Hebrew word is *Slav* and there is general agreement about the translation, although the fact that the birds are said to have lain three feet thick upon the earth over a circle two days' journey in diameter led some nineteenth-century naturalists to look for a more substantial bird, and the sand grouse, the Shelduck, and even the White Stork were suggested, in attempts to reduce the miraculous to the more easily credible.

Flights of Quail were known to migrate in huge quantities across Bible lands. Pliny mentions that they were so numerous as to constitute a danger to shipping:

> As touching quails, they always come before the cranes depart. Their manner of flying is in troops; but not without some danger of the sailors, when they approach near to land. For oftentimes they settle in great numbers on their sails, and there perch, which they do evermore in the night, and with their poise, bear down barks and small vessels, and finally sink them.

It is interesting that the account in Exodus is preceded by the words 'at night', because Quails, as noted by Pliny, do migrate at night.

The Quail (*Coturnix coturnix*) is still recorded today in Bible lands as a common passage migrant, which may well turn itself into a resident. They fly across the land in the spring and autumn, pausing for rest on the southern coasts where, for generations, they have been caught in nets for sale in the markets of the cities. The Quail is the smallest game bird and the only one that migrates. Secretive by day, only its occasional call 'wet-my-lips' gives away its position. It is almost impossible to flush and the Quail photograph here was much the most difficult to obtain.

Quail (*Coturnix coturnix*)

'And it came to pass that at even the quails came up and covered the camp.' (Exodus 16:13)

R AVEN

Brown-necked Raven
(*Corvus ruficollis*)

'And the ravens brought
him bread and flesh in
the morning...' (1 Kings
17:6)

There are eleven references, ten in the Old and one in the New Testament. The Hebrew word is *Oreb*, and the Greek *Corax*. The translation is not disputed. The Raven is the first bird to be mentioned in the Bible: it was sent out by Noah from the Ark to see if the waters had abated (Gen 8:7). It was not allowed as food by Mosaic law (Lev 11:15). Ravens brought food to the prophet Elijah by the brook Cherith (1 Kings 17:4-6) and they are expressly mentioned as indications of God's protective love (Job 38:41; Luke 12:24 and Psa 147:9). Together with the owl and the Bittern, they mark the desolation of Edom (Isaiah 34:11); the black locks of the beloved are compared to the glossy jet of the Raven's plumage (S. of S. 5:11); and there is a macabre illusion to the Raven's habit of attacking the eyes of corpses in Proverbs 30:17.

Ravens were regarded as birds of destiny or omen by the Romans, having been found on Egyptian and Assyrian monuments; but their use in the Bible is mainly as agents of, or symbols for, Divine protection. As a consequence of its role in the Ark, the Raven was thought to be able to smell land at a great distance, and Ravens were often taken on early voyages of exploration. In Hebrew legend, the Raven was cursed by Noah for refusing at the first request to leave the Ark in search of land. He has the reputation of being unkind to his young, which is why God has taken them under his special protection and arranges that for the first three days after their birth, when the parents totally neglect them, maggots spring from the parents' dung so that they have food until the time that their feathers turn black and they are cared for by their parents. The Raven has also a moral for mankind: it is said that he used to walk as normally as the other birds, but wanted to step as gracefully as the dove, so he gave up his old way of walking and tried to imitate the dove. He almost broke his bones in the attempt and then, being mocked by other birds, tried to revert to his original way of walking, but he had forgotten, and now hops and steps clumsily. So he is a parable for the discontented: he who is dissatisfied with his lot in life may well lose what little he has if he tries to take what properly belongs to others.

The AV translators were persuaded by their naturalists that the Raven had astonishing magical powers. Albertus Magnus, in his work *Of the Virtues of Animals*, wrote:

> If a raven's eggs be boiled and put again in the nest, straightway the raven goes to a certain island in the Red Sea ... and brings a stone with which it touches its eggs and immediately they become raw as they were before. It is wonderful that the boiled eggs should be revived. Now, if that stone be set in a ring with a laurel leaf under it, and a man bound with chains of a closed gate be touched [therewith], straightway the bound shall be loosened and the gate opened. And if that stone be put in the ear, it gives understanding of all birds. This stone is of diverse colours, and causes all anger to be forgotten.

The Raven (*Corvus corax*), which is the largest of the crow family, is a fairly rare resident in the Bible lands today, although the Brown-necked Raven (*Corvus ruficollis*) is frequently seen. It is very like a buzzard in outline, with a large, wedge-shaped tail and rather square-ended wings. It often soars, like a buzzard, to great heights and has a marvellously acrobatic flight display in which it can tumble, swoop, nose-dive, and even fly upside down, calling as it does so with a sound that the field guides variously write as 'pruk, pruk', 'grok', 'cruk', 'whow' and 'grog'!

It eats small mammals, which it hunts and kills, but also, and particularly in Bible lands, carrion: dead lambs and the placentas of sheep. It can live in a wide range of habitats from mountain to desert and sea coast. Usually it nests in rocky crags, though its large, untidy assembly of branches and twigs is sometimes seen close to the tops of larger trees.

Satyr

Satyr

'Their houses shall be full of doleful creatures . . . and satyrs shall dance there.' (Isaiah 13:21)

Used only by the prophet Isaiah in speaking of the destruction of Babylon and Idumea. 'Their houses', he writes, 'shall be full of doleful creatures; and owls shall dwell there and satyrs shall dance there' (Isaiah 13:21). And later, 'The wild beasts of the desert shall also meet with the wild beasts of the island and the satyr shall cry to his fellow' (Isaiah 34:14).

The Hebrew word is *Sa'ir*, and it means literally 'hairy one'. The zoologists, ever keen to claim as their own any creature in the Bible, have suggested that the word must refer to the great dog-headed baboons (*Papio*) of Egypt and Arabia, since these have been found on Egyptian monuments and the tale is that they were brought north from Africa to Egypt where they became objects of worship. But there is no reason to reject the mythological content here: Isaiah was not given to writing flat literalisms. It was accepted that one characteristic of desolate places was that demons came to inhabit them; and it was characteristic of satyrs that they danced in groups and cried out. So, although we cannot assume that the Hebrew notions of satyr contained all that the Greeks brought to the fabulous creature, it does seem reasonable to assume that what is intended here is a wild creature, half-man, half-goat, that danced and wailed at night over scenes of ruin and desolation.

S CORPION

One of the very few creatures that are given equal place in the Old and New Testaments. They inhabit and make more terrible the desert wilderness: 'Who led thee through that great and terrible wilderness wherein were fiery serpents and scorpions' (Deut 8:15), they are called onto a picture of desolation and danger: 'Be not afraid of them ... though briers and thorns be with thee and thou dost dwell among scorpions' (Ezek 2:6). And immunity from scorpions was one of the gifts promised by Christ to the Apostles: 'Behold, I give you power to tread on serpents and scorpions' (Luke 10:19). In the revelation of St John, the Locusts which would crawl out of the smoke in the bottomless pit would be equipped with 'tails like unto scorpions' (Rev 9:10) and they would inflict 'torment as the torment of a scorpion when he striketh a man' (Rev 9:5) and they would be given 'power, as the scorpions of the earth have power' (Rev 9:3). The pain inflicted by the sting of a scorpion is used in the powerful image 'My father hath chastised you with whips, but I will chastise you with scorpions' (1 Kings 12:11 and 2 Chron 10:14), and, in contrast, Christ portrays the love of God in the words, addressed to those who pray 'if he ask an egg, will he offer him a scorpion?' (Luke 11:12).

The Hebrew word is *Akrab*, the Greek *Scorpios* and there is no dispute about the translation. There are, after all, few creatures with which man comes into contact that leave so lasting an impression. There is a Hebrew legend that the wicked are tormented, after death, by scorpions in a place which is the habitation of scorpions. The brothers of Joseph, having stripped him naked, flung him into a pit of scorpions; scorpions were conjured up by the magical arts of Balaam to protect the capital city of King Kikanos; and the Israelites, during the period of their obedience to the laws of Moses, were protected by God from the scorpions in the desert.

Scorpion (*Scorpio maurus kruglovi*)

'Who led thee through that great and terrible wilderness wherein were fiery serpents and scorpions.' (Deuteronomy 8:15)

The legends attaching to scorpions in AV times had to do mainly with ways in which to allay the pain of the sting. Topsell, in his *Four-footed Beasts*, says:

> It is thought that hares are never molested by scorpions because if a man or beast be annointed with the rennet of a hare, there is no scorpion or spider that will hurt him. Wild goats are also said to live without fear of scorpions. The seed of nose wort burnt or scorched doth drive away serpents and resist scorpions and so doth the seed of violets and of wild parsnip. The smell of garlic or wild mints set on fire or strewed on the ground and dittany have the same operations; and above all other one of those scorpions burned driveth away all his fellows that are within the smell thereof ... To conclude, the spittle of a man is death unto scorpions.

Others recommend the eating of basil, but Lupton, in his *Notable Things*, has a stern warning about this:

> An Italian, through the oft smelling of an herb called Basil, had a Scorpion bred in his brain, which did not only a long time grieve him, but also at the last killed him. Jacobus Hollerius, a learned physician, affirms it for truth. Take heed, therefore, ye smellers of Basil.

134

The *Scorpionida*, or scorpions, are an order of the arachnid class: terrestrial animals with a body divided into two parts, for the most part oviparous, with periods of development in the larval and the nymphal stages. This class also includes mites and ticks and spiders. Scorpions are long arachnids, the abdomen normally having twelve segments, the last six of which form a tail which ends in the sting. They can vary from half an inch to eight inches in length, and in colour from red and brown through yellow to greyish white, or even, by contrast, a slate black.

S CREECH OWL

Barn Owl (*Tyto alba*)

'The screech owl also shall rest there and find for herself a place of rest.' (34:14)

In the description of the desolation which gathers together the wild beasts of the desert and the wild beasts of the island, the prophet Isaiah continues that 'the satyr shall cry to his fellows; the screech owl also shall rest there' (Isaiah 34:14). And it has been assumed by the natural historians, including Canon Tristram, that the bird referred to is that known in Britain as the Screech or Barn Owl (*Tyto alba*).

The Hebrew word is *Lilit*. It is interesting that modern translators, who for the most part are keen to find a word that has a counterpart in nature, have here abandoned the attempt.

NAS, AB and GNB all have 'night monster', the last giving a footnote that explains the monster in question is 'a female demon believed to live in desolate places'; RAV has 'night creatures' as does NIV; NEB has 'night jar' and JB does not attempt a translation, but leaves the Hebrew word as a proper name 'Lilith'.

The association with SATYRS (q.v.) does encourage a mythological rather than a naturalistic interpretation here, and Lilith was an established character in Hebrew mythology. She was the first wife of Adam, created, like him, from the dust of the ground. But she left him because he refused her demand for full rights of equality with him. Adam complained to God that his wife had deserted him and God sent three angels to search for her. They found her in the Red Sea and threatened that if she did not return to her husband she would lose a hundred of her demon children every day. She chose to accept this punishment rather than return to Adam, but takes her revenge by strangling babies during the first night of their lives. There is a tradition that Jews place coins in the bedrooms of their children inscribed with the names of the three angels who were sent by God, or with the names of Adam and Eve, to protect their children, and it is said that the word 'lullaby' is derived from the Hebrew *Lila abi*, or *Lilith avaunt*, although this is folk etymology, not recognised by the OED.

S HEEP

The most important animal in the Bible in both a literal and figurative sense. There are about 500 references including RAM and EWE. Sheep were the main possessions of the people of Bible lands and the chief measure of their prosperity. Abraham, Isaac, Jacob and Esau all had vast flocks of them and they were the biblical equivalent of a credit rating. They were also a medium of exchange, and the King of Moab paid an annual tribute of 100,000 lambs and the same number of rams to the King of Israel (2 Kings 8:4); Solomon sacrificed 120,000 sheep at the dedication of the temple (1 Kings 8:53) and 100 sheep a day were brought to his table (1 Kings 4:23). Wool was used for clothing (Lev 8:47; Deut 22:11; Prov 31:13;

Job 31:20) and 'rams' skins dyed red' were used as the covering for the Tabernacle (Exod 25:5). There is mention of sheep-shearing, which seems to have been a festival on a par with the harvest festival, in Genesis 31:19, Deuteronomy 15:19, 1 Samuel 25:4, and also of sheep dogs, though not as trained and obedient as those of our own time.

As the most valuable of the generally available animals, sheep were much called for in sacrifice; either the adult (Exod 20:24; 1 Kings 8:63; 2 Chron 29:33), or the young lambs (Exod 29:38; Lev 9:3; Num 28:9), although no lamb less than eight days old was permitted as a sacrifice (Lev 22:27).

The care of the sheep was so much a part of the everyday experience of people that the most powerful image of the relationship between God and his chosen folk was that of the shepherd with his flock. The shepherd would tend to go before his sheep, calling them to follow him (Psa 23; Psa 77:20; Psa 80:1), although there is one possible reference to the more familiar procedure of our own times when the shepherd drives the sheep before him (Gen 33:13). The shepherd collects the sheep in caves to protect them from the bad weather and wild beasts (1 Sam 24:3) or builds sheepfolds to guard them (Num 32:16; Judges 5:16) and will give his life for them (John 10:15), a situation strange to us, but familiar in days when the predators of the flock were likely to be Leopard, Lion, bear, or

Watering sheep and donkeys

'My sheep wandered through all the mountains and upon every high hill.' (Ezekiel 34:6)

Wolf. Another practice which is unfamiliar to our own shepherds, who tend to handle thousands of sheep in large and wide-ranging flocks, is that of knowing the names of the individual sheep (John 10:3) and, even more strange, of the sheep's knowing and recognising his voice (John 10:4). This practice is continued today only by smallholders.

In biblical times, if a number of flocks was brought together to be watered at a single fountain or waterhole, it was the practice for the shepherds to bring them together to lie and wait their turn, and then for the flocks to be called up one at a time, in turn, to drink. In the imagery of the Bible, the people of God are his sheep (Psa 95:7; 100:3; John 21:15-17) and his ministers are their pastors, that is their shepherds (Jer 23:1; Eph 4:1). And, when the risen Christ gave his commission to Peter, the image he used was that of the great tradition: 'Feed my sheep' (John 21:16-17). Christ is himself the 'Good Shepherd' (John 10:11) and the Lamb of God that taketh away the sins of the world (John 1:19). The final act of redemption is the marriage of the lamb (Rev 19:9; 21:9, 14).

The characteristics of the sheep that made them suitable as images of the people under God's care were noted in AV times by the naturalist Bartholomew: 'The sheep is a nesh [that is, soft] beast and beareth wool and is unarmed in body and pleasing in heart ... Also in sheep is less wit and understanding than in another four-footed beast.'

S NAIL

Included with the unclean creatures, 'the lizard, the snail, and the mole' of Leviticus 11:30, where the Hebrew word used is *Homet* and all modern translators have agreed that a form of lizard is meant. The zoologist Shulov identifies this creature with the skink, also known as the sand fish, the Cylindrical Skink (*Chalcides lineatus*) being found in the western Mediterranean and in the subdesert regions as far east as Pakistan. They are thick, squat animals with short powerful feet which they use to dig into the sand. The Cylindrical Skink can run in the normal way on these feet, but, if it wants to increase its speed, it can tuck them up into small recesses in the body

Roman Snail (*Helix pomatia*) (Photograph: Frank Lane)

'As a snail which melteth, let every one of them pass away.' (Psalm 58:8)

and glide along the surface like a snake. It feeds on insects and small molluscs and is oviparous.

The second reference to the snail is a telling image in Psalms: speaking of the wicked who are 'estranged from the womb', the psalmist cries 'As a snail which melteth, let every one of them pass away' (Psa 58:8). Here the Hebrew word used is *Shavluv*, which is clearly one of the genus *Helix*. In Hebrew lore, the snail was an example of the way that God's creatures all had a purpose on the earth, no matter how insignificant they may appear to be, and the snail, which loses its vitality in the moist streak which it leaves as it moves along is nevertheless significant because it is a cure for boils. And when Jacob sent Benjamin with presents into Egypt, the one which it was supposed would excite the greatest admiration was the *Murex*, the snail from which the dye of Tyrian purple is made.

The AV translators would have felt both that the snail was unclean, and that it dissolves into slime, since the naturalist Bartholomew had written: 'Snail is a worm of slime and breedeth of slime and is therefor alway foul and unclean; and is a manner of snake, and is an horned worm. And such worms be gendered principally in corrupt air and rain.' The more highly principled of them might well have agreed with the Hebrews that the snail has a purpose since Lupton, in his *Notable Things*, advised that 'The two horns of a snail born upon a man will pluck away carnal or fleshly lust from the bearer thereof.'

There are 68 species of the family *Helicidae* in the area of the Bible lands, where the limestone rocks provide calcium for the shells. Because the text refers to the trail of slime left behind by the creature, and because we are more familiar with this trail in connection with the slug, two of the modern translations prefer the word 'slug' (NIV and JB). In fact, a slug is simply the common name given to snails which have lost, or appear to have lost, their shells, and since the process of shell reduction in different species is continuous between the obvious presence and the total absence of shell, the line is hard to draw between snail and slug. Probably the modern reader with experience of vegetable gardening would find the image of the slug the more familiar.

S PARROW

The Hebrew word translated as 'sparrow' in the AV occurs over 40 times in the Old Testament: *Zipor*, which means basically to chirp or twitter, is commonly translated as either 'bird' or 'fowl' and clearly refers to what bird-watchers have come to call the 'small brown jobs', that is, any one of the many small passerines that are predominantly brown in colour and easily confused. There are, however, two specific references to the sparrow in the Old Testament, and four in the New. The psalmist, singing to the sons of Korah of the joys of the solicitude of the living God, cries 'Yea, the sparrow hath found an house and the swallow a nest for herself, where she may lay her young ...' (Psa 84:3), and in the contrasting prayer of the afflicted he conjures up a striking image of the lonely sufferer: 'I watch and am as a sparrow alone upon the house top' (Psa 102:7). This last image has led many naturalists, from Tristram to the present time, to suggest that the bird referred to by the psalmist cannot be the sparrow, since it is most commonly seen in flocks. They have substituted the Blue Rock Thrush (*Monticola solitarius*), more noted for its solitary habits as the species name implies. The suggestion has its merits but for the general reader the more common name makes the image more telling.

In the words of Christ which reassure the disciples of their worth in the eyes of God, he reveals something of the practices

House Sparrow (*Passer domesticus*)

'I watch and am as a sparrow alone upon the housetop.' (Psalm 102:7)

of his time: 'Are not two sparrows sold for a farthing? . . . ye are of more value than many sparrows' (Matt 10:29-31). Sparrows were caught in traps and then carried around the houses by small boys, ready plucked to be grilled and eaten, and the reference in Luke to the same image, which reads 'Are not five sparrows sold for two farthings?' (Luke 12:6) suggests that, if you bought four sparrows at the rate of two for a farthing, you were given a free one in recognition of a bulk purchase. The practice of trapping or snaring birds is mentioned in Proverbs, where we are told that 'surely, in vain the net is spread in the sight of any bird' (Prov 1:17), and the snare, the trap and the gin are all mentioned in Job 18:8-10. But there was a sensitivity from the earliest biblical times to the needs of conservation, and we find a caution in Deuteronomy 22:6 that the adult birds must never be taken as well as the nestlings or the eggs.

According to Jewish lore the sparrow, moulded in gold, stands on the throne of Solomon and, through an ingenious piece of machinery, would chirp as the king set his foot on the first of the steps leading up to it. The AV translators would have felt this an inappropriate bird for such a position, since the naturalist Bartholomew had told them that

The sparrow is an unsteadfast bird with voice and jangling, and is a full hot bird and lecherous, and the flesh of them oft taken in meat exciteth to carnal lust. Sparrows lay many eggs and are full busy to bring up their birds, and to feed them. And she keepeth her nest clean without dirt, and therefore she throweth the dirt of her birds out of the nest, and compelleth her birds to throw their dirt out of the nest; and they feed their birds with attercops [spiders], worms and flies; and they eat venomous seeds, as of henbane without hurt; and they have sometimes leprosy and the falling evil.

They did, however, have one virtue unexploited in our own time: Lupton points out in *Notable Things* that 'If any will make their hands white, let them mix the dung of sparrows in warm water, and wash them therewith.'

Bible lands today are rich in the sparrow family: there are, as common residents, the Spanish Sparrow (*Passer hispaniolensis*), and the House Sparrow (*Passer domesticus*). The Dead Sea Sparrow (*Passer moabiticus*) is occasionally seen as an accidental; the Rock Sparrow (*Petronia petronia*) commonly spends the summer months there, as does, more rarely, the Pale Rock Sparrow (*Petronia brachydactyla*).

S PIDER

In two of the three references, the text makes use of the spider's web as an image of something insubstantial, of no value, and easily destroyed: 'The hypocrite's hope shall perish: whose hope shall be cut off and whose trust shall be a spider's web' (Job 8:14) and Isaiah speaks of the futile plotting of the unjust as 'they weave the spider's web' (Isaiah 59:5). That a spider's web is so flimsy as to be of no lasting value is generally accepted today, although a certain M. Bon of Montpellier became, for a time, famous in the eighteenth century for boasting stockings and gloves woven from spiders' silk, and there have been recent attempts to revive the art.

In Hebrew lore the spider was yet another example of an apparently futile creature having a purpose: David one day expressed his doubt of God's wisdom in having created such a useless creature as a spider that busies itself spinning a web that has no value. But when he was being pursued by Saul and took refuge in a cave, God sent a spider to weave its web across the opening and Saul called his men away from the

Black Widow Spider (*Latrodectus mectans*)

'The hypocrites hope shall perish... whose trust shall be a spiders web.' (Job 8:14)

cave, saying that it was useless to search within, since the web showed that no one could have entered. So David's life was saved by the tiny creature he had scorned.

Spiders were widely thought to be poisonous in AV times, Bartholomew having assured his readers that:

> The venomous spider is a little creeping beast with many feet, and hath vi feet or viii, and hath alway feet even and not odd; and that is very needful that his going and passing be alway even ... Against all biting of spiders, the remedy is the brain of a capon drunk in sweet wine with a little pepper; also flies stamped and laid to the biting draweth out the venom and abateth the ache and sore. And the same doth the ashes of a ram's claw with honey.

Spiders, of course, have eight legs and though many are venomous, the strength of the venom is, in only a few species, sufficient to be hurtful to man. They are very common in Bible lands, although as elsewhere their webs are far more frequently seen than the spiders themselves. In the two references above the Hebrew word is *Akavis*, and there is general agreement on the translation. There is a third OT reference: 'The spider taketh hold with her hands, and is in kings' palaces' (Prov 30:28), where the Hebrew word used is *Smamit*, which most translators now agree is probably a small lizard (see GECKO).

S TORK

White Stork (*Ciconia ciconia*)

'Yea the stork in the heaven knoweth her appointed times.' (Jeremiah 8:7)

Included among the birds which are to be held in abomination among the fowls (Lev 11:19 and Deut 14:18), but otherwise a bird held up for some admiration by the prophets: Jeremiah, reproving a people who have left the ways of the Lord, contrasts them with the bird which follows the rules of its existence: 'Yea the stork in heaven knoweth her appointed times' (Jer 8:7), that is, she knows the season for migration and duly takes to the high air and flies away. The great power and beauty of the stork's wings, which carry it at great heights on its long migrations were also noticed: 'The wind was in their wings, for they had wings like the wings of a stork' (Zech 5:9). And the habit of the stork of choosing the tallest of the trees strong enough to accommodate its huge nest is noted: 'as for the stork, the fir trees are her house' (Psa 104:17).

The Hebrew word is *Hasidah* and the translation is generally agreed. The stork was a familiar sight in Bible lands, both in nature, as a familiar spring passage migrant, and in folklore. The literal meaning of the Hebrew name is 'the pious one' and storks were legendary for their kindness to each other and for the purity and loyalty of their family life. The Romans also called the stork *pia avis* (the pious bird). They were regarded as models of behaviour for humanity and boxes were placed on the roofs of houses to try to encourage the stork to come and nest. There is a legend that Moses taught the people of Ethiopia, when besieging a city guarded by serpents, to train young storks to fly as hawks and then, having starved them for three days, to release them over the city whereupon the storks killed all the serpents and the city was taken.

In AV times, storks were known to have this enmity for serpents, feeding their young on the bodies of adders, and they were also the only birds reputed to recognise and care for their own parents in old age. They also had strong views on the purity of domestic life. As Bartholomew records: 'While the female liveth, the male keepeth truly to her in nest. And if the male espy, in any wise, that the female hath broken spousehead, she shall no more dwell with him, but he beateth and striketh her with his bill, and slayeth her, if he may.'

There are two storks to be found in Bible lands today: the White Stork (*Ciconia ciconia*) is recorded as a common passage migrant, occasionally overwintering there, and the Black Stork (*Ciconia nigra*), which also occasionally overwinters, is rare but also a passage migrant.

SWALLOW

The references to this bird, all in the OT, speak of well-established habits which the writers must have noted from observation: their way of building nests, their migrations, their flight, and their calling. 'The swallow hath found a nest for herself, even thine altars, O Lord of Hosts' (Psa 84:3) refers to the birds' frequent habit of nesting in houses and temples, close to human habitation. 'The turtle, the crane and the swallow observe the time of their coming' (Jer 8:7) notes the regularity with which Swallows return with the spring; and the constant chattering note of the Swallow, which made it a byword for garrulity among the Greeks, is observed in 'Like a crane or a swallow, so did I chatter' (Isaiah 38:14).

There is a rather puzzling reference in Proverbs: 'as the swallow by flying, so the curse causeless shall not come' (Pro 26:2), which seems to mean that a curse which is undeserved will not settle on, or harm anyone, but fly past them as the Swallow which flies by and does not land. In this instance, the

Swallow (*Hirundo rustica*) at sunset

'The turtle and the crane and the swallow observe the time of their coming.' (Jeremiah 8:7)

Swift, which spends a far greater proportion of its time on the wing, would be a better image.

The Hebrew word is *Dero* and the translation agreed, though some commentators have suggested that the Swift or the House Martin would fit equally well. There is no reason to challenge the translation and there was a tradition, known in AV times, that Swallows chattered to each other constantly in flight, which is why a broth of crushed Swallows was a recommended cure of the times for epilepsy or stammering. The Swallow (*Hirundo rustica*) is a common migrant still in Bible lands, and its relatives the Crag Martin (*Ptyonoprogne rupestris*) and the Red-rumped Swallow (*Hirundo daurica*) are also recorded there.

S WAN

Only recorded in the list of unclean birds: 'And these are they which ye shall have in abomination . . . and the swan and the pelican and the gier eagle' (Lev 11:13-19 and Deut 14:16).

The Hebrew word is *Tinshemet* and there is great dispute about the translation, impossible to resolve because it is found nowhere else. Modern zoologists have suggested both the Purple Gallinule (*Porphyrio porphyrio*) and the Barn owl (*Tyto alba*), and the modern translators have a wide variety, only RAV keeping 'swan'. NIV has 'white owl', NEB has 'Little owl', RV has 'Horned owl', and RSV 'water hen'. What they all seem to agree on is that 'swan' is wrong. Bewick's Swan and the Whooper and Mute Swan have been recorded in recent times in Bible lands, but they are very rarely seen there.

Little Owl (*Athena noctua*)

S WINE

They are mentioned six times in the OT, always with horror, and 14 times in the NT, where the revulsion seems to be less. The Hebrew word is *Chazir*, the Greek *Choiros*; there is no dispute about the translation. Swine are best known in the Bible context for the fact that they were an abomination to the Jews. Their meat was forbidden (Lev 11:7 and Deut 14:8) because they have cloven feet but do not chew the cud, and the habit which pigs have of stretching out their feet as they lie down was noticed by the ancient Hebrews as a sign that the animal was trying to show its cloven hoof in an attempt to be accepted as a clean animal. But pigs were not only forbidden meat, they were not to be touched by the scrupulous; some went so far as to avoid mentioning the name, calling the pig 'that unclean thing'. There are proverbs which stress the horror in which the swine was held by the faithful, in utter contrast with that which is clean, wholesome and good: 'As a jewel of gold in a swine's snout, so is a fair woman which is without discretions' (Prov 11:22) and 'Neither cast ye your pearls before swine, lest they trample them under their feet' (Matt 7:6). And Christians who have known the truth and fallen away from it are compared by St Peter to the dogs that return to their own vomit or 'the swine that was washed to her wallowing in the mire' (2 Pet 2:22).

The Jews fell away, in OT times, from their strict adherence to the Mosaic prohibition and Isaiah speaks of a rebellious people 'which eat swine's flesh and broth of abominable things' (Isaiah 65:4). The prophet also declares that on the day when the Lord shall come with fire and like a whirlwind, all the idolators who are found 'eating swine's flesh and the abomination and the mouse shall be consumed together' (Isaiah 65:4). But clearly there were herds of swine kept in the Holy Land in the time of Christ, since he tells the story of the prodigal son who was employed to feed them (Luke 15) and permitted the devils to enter the bodies of the Gadarene swine as told in Matthew 8, Mark 5, and Luke 8.

The intensity of the abomination of pork is illustrated in the Book of Maccabees; as a sign that he had rejected the faith of his fathers, the old man Eleazar was forced to put swine's flesh into his mouth. 'He, choosing to die gloriously, rather than live stained with such an abomination, spit it forth and came of his own accord to the torment' (2 Macc 6:18). The basis of this extreme abomination of the pig has been variously interpreted. Those who like to find a reasonable or scientifically respectable foundation for apparently irrational conduct explain that the flesh of pigs tends to harbour parasites which are prevalent in hotter climates and that these are easily transferred to humans if the meat is not properly cooked. Although many still believe this, and so we are served the grey and dried up pork which is felt to be·safe by timid restaurateurs, the pig is eaten with delight and festivity throughout the South Sea islands, cooked on hot stones in earth ovens, often to the degree of rare steak and, indeed, at this temperature it is perfectly safe.

The explanation on grounds of dietary hygiene does not, of course, explain the revulsion felt for the living animal, and this seems to be far more probably explained by an ancient taboo. Scholars have suggested that the pig was taboo to the ancient Egyptians because it turned up the earth with its snout and so first taught man to plough. Certainly it was believed that the souls of the wicked migrated into pigs, and this would account for a refusal to eat the flesh in case the wickedness could be passed on through the tainted pork. What is perfectly clear is that the abomination of the swine is too severe to be explained by reference to internal parasites or hazards to health, and must be put down to the laws of taboo which were passed on through the Egyptians.

Tamworth Cross Pig

'As a jewel of gold in a swine's snout, so is a fair woman which is without discretion.' (Proverbs 11:22)

TORTOISE

Only mentioned among the unclean animals that creep upon the earth (Lev 11:29).

The Hebrew word is *Tsav* and the translation is disputed. There were early attempts by commentators to connect this with an Arabic word *Dab*, which means the spiny-tailed lizard, and the modern versions prefer 'lizard' here, although the word occurs in the next verse and, since there is an abundance of tortoises in Bible lands, there seems no overwhelming reason to abandon the AV translation. It would certainly not be an attractive food and, both in appearance and behaviour, would seem to be properly classified as one of the creeping things that creep upon the earth, and so unclean. The tortoise, although a fairly primitive animal, has been a remarkable biological success with a great resistance to disease and a capacity to thrive in a wide variety of harsh conditions in spite of being the favourite food of several birds of prey, and having its eggs cooked and eaten by man.

Tortoise (*Testudo graeca*)

UNICORN

Unicorn

'Will the unicorn be willing to serve thee, or abide by thy crib?' (Job 39:9)

There are nine references, some of which are in contexts which seem to fight against the AV translation: it is an animal characterised by great strength (Num 23:22 and 24:8); it is associated with bullocks and bulls (Isaiah 34:7); it is used in agriculture (Job 39:9-12); and, in Deuteronomy 33:17, all modern translators agree that the context specifies it has more than one horn, the correct translation being 'his horns are the horns of a unicorn'.

The Hebrew word is *Reem*, and it was changed to 'wild ox' as early as the RV. All modern translations follow this. There is, however, a mythological animal of this name recorded in the legends of the Jews. It was a giant animal, of which only one pair was allowed to be in existence at a time, otherwise they would have tyrannised the world. God ordained that they should meet and breed only once in 70 years, and for the rest of their time they inhabit opposite ends of the earth. The female remains pregnant for twelve years, at the end of which time she gives birth to twins, a male and a female, always dying in the act. As soon as they are born, one turns to the east and the other to the west and they journey away from each other, to meet again only after 70 years.

It is also said that when Adam first saw a sunset he was afraid that the darkness would cover the earth permanently and the end of the world had come; so he sacrificed to God a unicorn, which had the special virtue of having a horn created before his hooves: as the beast emerged from the primordial mud, it put out its head first, with the horn already formed on it.

By the time of the AV translation, the belief in unicorns was losing its grip among the educated, as witness Shakespeare's introducing references to them in both *Timon of Athens* (Act 4 Scene 3:14) and *Julius Caesar* (Act 2 Scene 1:19), but then having Sebastian, in *The Tempest*, reacting to the magical scenes shown by Prospero with the words: 'A living drollery! Now will I believe that there are unicorns' (Act 3 Scene 3:122). In the 1616 edition of Purchas's *Pilgrims*, it is recorded that 'Of the unicorn, none hath been seen these hundred years past', although Sir Thomas Browne, in his *Vulgar Errors* affirms the existence of unicorns and Topsell, in his *Four-footed Beasts* attacks those who do not believe in the existence of unicorns, suggesting that their scepticism is close to atheism.

So much for the background of beliefs. It seems most probably that the *Reem* of scriptures combined mythological and natural elements.

VIPER

It is very interesting that the biblical use of the word 'viper' follows closely the colloquial use in English, namely that it means any poisonous snake. There is no scriptural allusion by which it would be possible to be certain about the identification of the snake called by the Hebrew word *Ephem*, which is from a root meaning simply to hiss, but the family of true vipers (*Viperidae*) is widespread, from Britain through Africa and across Asia to China.

'The viper's tongue shall slay him' (Job 20:16) is clearly a figure of speech rather than a literal prophecy, since the tongue of the viper, though menacing, is harmless. It is simply a smell-taste organ which flicks in and out of the mouth to pick up particles of air which are then carried back for analysis inside the head. Isaiah names the snake twice, 'The viper and the fiery serpent' in 30:6, and 'that which is crushed breaketh out into a viper' in 59:5, a reference which seems to imply that something stepped on in the sand, some half-hidden object, turns out to be a snake. Here the moderns vary between those who retain viper, those who prefer snake, and the NEB which specifies 'Sand viper', possibly because of this context.

In the NT the Greek word is *Echidna*, and those in the synoptic gospels, are figures of speech, the 'viper's brood' of Matthew 3:7, 12:34, 23:33, and Luke 3:7 which is a term of abuse for the unbelievers, who were numerous and death-dealing. The only other reference to the viper is the one which fastened itself on the hand of St Paul, when he was collecting firewood in Malta (Acts 23:3). This could have been the Common Viper (*Vipera berus*) or the more easily concealed Aspic Viper (*Vipera aspis*). Neither exists in Malta today, but their extinction could well have been brought about by the destruction of habitat since New Testament times. It is not essential to identify the species, of course: all St Luke meant to convey was that the snake was known to be poisonous, since, when the barbarous people saw that St Paul did not fall down dead from the bite, they decided he must be a god.

Palestine Viper (*Vipera xanthina*)

'There came a viper out of the heat, and fastened on his hand.' (Acts 28:3)

In Hebrew legend, the viper was instanced as a member of a chain of creatures which seem to be either useless or noxious, and yet are evidence of God's goodness, in that they each have their purpose. So the gnat, which is so tiny that it eats but does not excrete its food, is a specific against the poison of the viper, and the viper itself is a cure for skin eruptions. In AV times it was recorded that 'Of this serpent be made pasties of the which is made treacle, that is remedy against venom ... Also if the dragon or the adder which is hight asp biteth a man or a beast, the head of the adder Viper healeth him and saveth him, if it be laid to the wound' (Bartholomew). Vipers were also known to be eaten as an antidote to leprosy, and the best known behavioural trait they had was inferred from the name, which is from the Latin *vipera*, itself a contraction of *vivipora*, meaning to bring forth alive and alluding to the belief that vipers gave birth to live young. Bartholomew records that this was because the young, when sufficiently mature, eat their way out of the mother's womb and kill her. There was also a common belief that the mother viper had the habit of protecting her young by swallowing them, if threatened, and letting them emerge from her mouth after danger had passed. This is recorded as early as Holinshed's *Chronicle* of 1577.

In fact, the viper is ovoviviparous: that is, they hatch the eggs inside the parent and then the five to twenty young emerge, each six to eight inches long. Some snakes lay eggs, some give birth to live young, and the gradation between them is so gradual that the subspecies of the Levantine Viper (*Vipera lebetina lebetina*), found in Cyprus, gives birth to live young, whereas the same subspecies living in Asia Minor and central Asia, lays eggs.

V ULTURE

Included among the fowl which are to be held in abomination under Mosaic law (Lev 11:14 and Deut 14:13), and also noted for the keenness of its vision 'There is a path which no fowl knoweth, and which the vulture's eye hath not seen' (Job 28:7). This reflects an ancient belief, recorded in the Talmud, that a vulture in Babylon could see a carcase in Palestine. And in the

vision of the destruction of Edom, when her rivers shall be turned into tar and her soil into sulphur, 'there shall the vultures also be gathered, every one with her mate' (Isaiah 34:15). The Hebrew word is *Aia* or *Daia*, and this has been connected with the Arabic *L'Dayah*, which means KITE (q.v.). However, the vulture is sufficiently well established in Bible lands to warrant its place in scripture, and the keenness of vision together with the habit of gathering in flocks where there is carrion both fit the contexts in which it occurs.

The vulture had a special role in Hebrew lore dealing with the last days, since it has the duty of announcing the coming of the Messiah, which it will accomplish by sitting on the ground and singing a hymn. Like so many creatures that were not easy to come across, and therefore whose mythical virtues could not easily be put to the test, the vulture was credited, by the naturalist Bartholomew, with magical healing powers:

Griffon Vulture (*Gyps fulvus*)

'There is a path which no fowl knoweth, and which the vulture's eye hath not seen.' (Job 28:7)

The heart thereof maketh a man safe that beareth it among serpents and wild beasts. The heart bound in a lion's skin or in a wolf's skin, driveth away fiends. His right foot bound to

155

the left foot healeth that acheth; the left foot also healeth the right foot. His tongue, plucked out with iron and hanged about a man's neck, in new cloth, maketh a man gracious to get of a man what he desireth.

The most common species of vulture in Bible lands is the Griffon Vulture (*Gyps fulvus*), frequently seen wheeling high in the sky and notable for its unusually pale colour, contrasting with dark wing feathers. The largest in the region is the Bearded Vulture, or Lammergeier (*Gypaetus barbatus*), which currently has the status of a rare resident. This bird tends not to join the others at the kill but remains aloof in the high mountains. It has the habit of dropping bones from great heights onto the rocks to break them into small pieces that it can eat, and is referred to in the AV name OSSIFRAGE (q.v.). The Lappet-faced Vulture (*Torgos tracheliotus*) and the Black Vulture (*Aegypius monachus*) are also found in the region, but very rarely, the former breeding there and the latter being a passage migrant. And the smallest of the family is the frequently seen summer migrant, the Egyptian Vulture (*Neophron percnopterus*), which is strongly contrasting in black and white colours and commonly found scavenging the rubbish tips of settled areas.

WEASEL

Included among the unclean creeping things that creep upon the earth in Leviticus 11:29 and not found elsewhere. The Hebrew word is *Holed* and, as the animal is not mentioned outside the list of the unclean, its identification is uncertain and some modern translators prefer 'Mole Rat' (see MOLE).

The weasel, however, would fit well the description of an animal that creeps upon the earth and there are a number of reasons why the Hebrews would think of them as unclean. According to Hebrew legend, the weasel is impregnated through the ears and gives birth through the mouth. This idea is mentioned by Aristotle in his *De Generatione Animalium*, but he scoffs at it. The notion has survived into AV times, however, and Bartholomew records:

The Weasel is, as it were, a long mouse. This beast hath a guileful wit and nourisheth her kittens, and beareth them from place to place, and changeth place and dwelling, for her nest should not be found. The weasel pursueth and eateth serpents and hateth and eateth mice. And their opinion is false that mean that weasels conceive at mouth, and kitteneth at the ear.

Like so many wild creatures, the weasel was thought to have medicinal properties. Albertus Magnus, in his *Of the Virtue of Animals*, records:

If the heart of a weasel be eaten while still palpitating, it makes a man know future events, and if any man eat of its heart with the eyes and tongue of a dog, he will forth with lose his voice.

The weasel found in Bible lands is the Common Weasel (*Mustela nivalis*), which ranges across Northern and Central Europe, varying greatly in size and colour. The slightly larger, but very similar Polecat (*Mustela putorius*), which could well be included under this Hebrew name, is also found there.

Weasel (*Mustela nivalis*)

WHALE

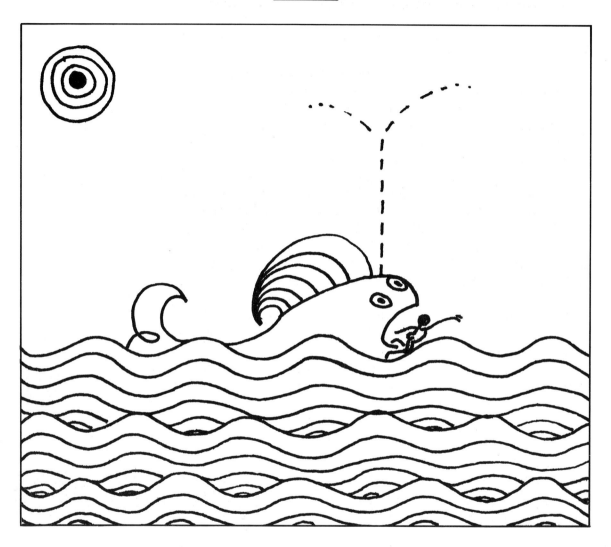

Whale

'Now the Lord had prepared a great fish to swallow up Jonah . . .' (Jonah 1:17)

There are three specific mentions in the AV, none of which enables a positive identification to be made. The prophet Ezekiel is called on by the Lord to take up a lamentation to the Pharaoh, king of Egypt and say unto him: 'Thou art like a young lion of the nations, and thou art as a whale in the seas' (Ezek 32:2), where the idea is clearly to indicate something of grandeur, but not necessarily a species of whale. In Genesis, we are told that 'God created great whales and every living creature that moveth' (Gen 1:21), and Job complains 'Am I a sea or a whale that thou settest a watch over me?' (Job 7:12).

The Hebrew word is *Tannin* and it is most frequently translated simply as 'sea monsters'. This is one of the few words for which the modern translators have preferred a mythical to a biological translation: NIV, NAB, RAV, and NAS all give 'monster', and RV has 'Dragon' for the references in Job and Ezekiel. The Genesis passage is variously translated; RAV and NAV have 'great creatures'; AB, NEB, NAS and GNB all have 'monsters'; JB has 'great sea serpents'. So the whale has completely disappeared from our modern translations.

The most famous whale in the Bible is, of course, the one that swallowed Jonah. But, in the book of Jonah itself, the creature is simply referred to as a 'great fish' (Jonah 1:17). When Christ refers to the story, however, he uses the name quite specifically: 'as Jonas was three days and three nights in the whale's belly, so the Son of Man shall be three days and three nights in the heart of the earth' (Matt 12:40). Here the Greek word is *Ketos*, which most moderns translate as 'sea monster' (as do JB, NEB, NAS and AB) with a minority following for 'big fish' (GNB), 'huge fish' (NIV) and 'great fish' (RAV). So, even here, the whale has been replaced.

There has been much argument about the species of fish which swallowed Jonah, but the arguments seem to ignore the text which says quite clearly that 'the Lord had prepared a great fish to swallow up Jonah' (Jonah 1:17). So the creature was not merely a natural species which happened to be passing: it was a miracle wrought by the Lord, for which it is futile to seek naturalistic explanations.

WILD ASS

Whereas the donkey was a possession of man and an indispensable beast of burden, the wild ass is a symbol of power and freedom: 'Who hath loosed the bonds of the wild ass?' (Job 39:5) and 'the range of the mountains is his pasture, and he searcheth after every green thing' (Job 39:6-8). 'A wild ass used to the wilderness that snuffeth up the wind at her pleasure' (Jer 2:24) and 'The wild asses did stand in the high places, they snuffed up the wind like dragons' (Jer 14:6). All the references seem to hint at a wild, untameable nature, with a

Asiatic Wild Ass and Foal
(*Equus hemionus*)

'The wild ass . . . that snuffeth up the wind at her pleasure.'
(Jeremaiah 2:24)

touch of admiration.

The Hebrew word is *Arod*, or *Pere*, and the animal was well known in Bible lands. The Asiatic Wild Ass (*Equus hemionus*) also known as the Onager, once ranged from Arabia to Tibet, grazing in large herds by day, under the leadership of a female, and sheltering in the shrubland at night. They still exist in the area and can gallop at speeds of up to 45 miles per hour for short distances. It could never be satisfactorily trained, which is why the name *Pere*, which means 'wild' was given to it. The same name is now used for any animal that cannot be domesticated. There was another species, the Syrian Wild Ass, in Bible times, but this is now thought to be extinct, the last specimens having been killed about 40 years ago by tribesmen from the north.

The Onager is protected and kept in the Hai-Bar Biblical Wildlife Reserve.

WILD GOAT

Allowed as meat by the list in Deuteronomy 14:5 and mentioned in the description of the hunting of David by Saul: 'Then Saul ... went to seek David and his men upon the hills of the wild goat' (1 Sam 24:2). As a creature of the wilderness, its habits are used to taunt Job in 'Knowest thou the time when the wild goats of the rock bring forth' (Job 39:1) and their dwelling in the inaccessible peaks of the mountains is an image for the psalmist: 'The high hills are a refuge for the wild goats' (Psa 104:18).

There are two Hebrew words used here: *Aku* in Deuteronomy and *Ye'elim* in the others. The ancestor of the Domestic Goat, *Capra hircus*, was found in Bible lands in ancient times, as evidenced by bone remains found among Stone Age deposits, but it had long been extinct before the days of the Old Testament and the creature referred to in all these references was, it is now agreed, the Nubian Ibex (see IBEX).

Nubian Ibex (*Capra nubiana*)

'The high hills are a refuge for the wild goats.' (Psalm 104:18)

161

Wolf

Negev or Judean Wolf (*Canis lupus*)

'Her judges are evening wolves; they gnaw not the bones till the morrow.' (Zephanaia 3:3)

There are 13 references to the Wolf, none of them flattering. As one of the main predators of the sole source of wealth of the people of Bible lands, Wolves were well known, easily recognised and therefore common as symbols or metaphors for destructive ravening power. 'Benjamin shall raven as a wolf', prophesies Genesis 49:27, and 'a wolf of the evenings shall spoil them' (Jer 5:6). The horses of Habakkuk and the judges of Zephaniah are 'as evening wolves' (Hab 1:8 and Zeph 3:3), and the sins of Jerusalem are condemned by Ezekiel with the words 'Her princes in the midst thereof are like wolves ravening the prey' (Ezek 22:27). The miracle to be wrought by the bringing about of the final harmony in the peaceable kingdom is evidenced by the change in the nature of the Wolf: 'The wolf also shall dwell with the lamb and the leopard shall lie down with the kid' (Isaiah 11:6) and 'The wolf and lamb shall feed together and the lion shall eat straw like a bullock'

(Isaiah 65:25). In the New Testament, Christ uses the savagery of the Wolf as an image of the dangers into which his disciples will be drawn: 'Behold, I send you forth as sheep in the midst of wolves' (Matt 10:16 and Luke 10:3); and he further warns, in words that have entered the language as a figure of speech: 'Beware of false prophets which come to you in sheep's clothing, but inwardly they are as ravening wolves' (Matt 7:15).

Christ, the good shepherd, who will lay down his life for the sheep, contrasts this with the attitude of the hireling who, 'seeth the wolf coming and leaveth the sheep and fleeth: and the wolf catcheth them and scattereth the sheep' (John 10:12). And finally, the words of the risen Christ: 'I know this, that after my departing shall grievous wolves enter in among you, not sparing the flock' (Acts 20:29).

The Hebrew word is *Zeeb*, the Greek *Lukos*; there is no dispute about the identity. Wolves are common in the folklore of pastoral nations as the creatures of evil and ill will. To the Hebrews, they figured in ancient legend: the Lord sent a plague of them among the Egyptians because the Egyptians had forced the Israelites in captivity to go out and capture Wolves and Lions for their circuses. Benjamin, youngest son of Jacob and Rachel, had the image of the Wolf on his flag, because his tribe was described by Jacob as 'like a wolf that raveneth'. And the Israelites themselves, in their invincibility, were likened to Wolves, Lions and serpents.

Wolves were creatures of the night with miraculous tales attached to them in AV times, as Topsell records in *Four-footed Beasts*:

The brains of a wolf do decrease and increase with the moon. The neck of a wolf is short, which argueth a treacherous nature. If the heart of a wolf be kept dry, it rendereth a most pleasant and sweet-smelling savour ... If a wolf treadeth in the footsteps of a horse which draweth a wagon, he cleaveth fast in the road as if he were frozen. The wolf is afraid of a sea crab or shrimp. If a man anoint himself with the fat or suet taken out of the reins of a lion, it will drive away from him all kinds of wolves ... If any labouring or travelling man doth wear the skin of a wolf about his feet, his shoes shall never pain or trouble him. He which will eat the skin of a wolf well tempered and sodden will keep him from all evil dreams and cause him to take his rest quietly. The teeth of a wolf being rubbed on the gums of young infants doth open them whereby the teeth may the easier come forth.

The form of Wolf found in Bible lands is the Grey Wolf (*Canis lupus*), which has a great variation in colouring, from a brownish to a yellowish grey, with flecks of black hair and lighter underparts. They are far smaller than the Wolves to the north, those of the Negev desert being on average about one-third the weight of the Alaskan Wolves. They have been protected by law since the 1950s and can still be seen in the wild, as well as being kept at the Hai-Bar Arava Biblical Wildlife Reserve.

WORM

In all of the 19 references, there is not one which clearly applies to the earthworm, although this is commonly found in Bible lands. The word is used, as it is commonly in our own speech, of lowly creeping things that are destructive. Bildad the Shuhite, one of Job's comforters, points out to him that even the stars are not pure in the sight of God. 'How much less Man, that is a worm? And the son of man, which is a worm?' (Job 25:6). Job's skin ailment he describes: 'My flesh is clothed with worms and clods of dust' (Job 7:5) which seems to imply entozoa of some kind; and he speaks of the destruction of his body after death in the familiar way: 'the worms shall cover him' (Job 21:26) and 'the worms shall feed sweetly on him' (Job 24:20).

When the children of Israel, against the express command of Moses, left manna overnight, it bred worms (Exod 16:20) and worms destroyed the vines in Deuteronomy 28:39. Future punishment, in pre-Christian times, was through fire and worms, and Isaiah speaks of the eternal nature of this in the words 'their worm shall not die, neither shall their fire be quenched' (Isaiah 66:24), a text to which Christ is clearly referring in Mark 9:48.

Commentators have drawn attention to the possible origins of this harrowing picture in the piles of rubbish that are found outside the towns and cities of Bible lands, which were kept continuously burning in an effort to dispose of them, and which were always, from the quantities of offal thrown out, seething with maggots.

For the most part, indeed, the worms seem to refer to maggots, which are the larvae of various fruit and flesh flies which eat putrefying vegetable and animal matter. The worms which caused the death of Herod could well have been symbolic of the fate of the unrighteous: from the legendary fate of Adam, worms have always been allowed at the bodies of the impious, as the faithful have been protected from them.

Maggots

'The worm shall feed sweetly on him; he shall be no more remembered.' (Job 24:20)

BIBLIOGRAPHY

ALON, Azaria. *The Natural History of the Land of the Bible*. Hamlyn, London, 1969

ARISTOTLE. *Historia Animalium* (transl. A.L. Peck). Loeb Classical Library, Heinemann, London, 1965

BARTHOLOMEW, 1535. *Bartholomeus de Proprietatibus Rerum* (transl. J. Trevisa). Quoted in SEAGER, 1896

BODENHEIMER, F.S. *Animal and Man in Bible Lands*. E.J. Brill, Leidon, 1960

CANSDALE, George. *Animals of Bible Lands*. Paternoster Press, Exeter, 1970

CLARK, Ann. *Beasts and Bawdy*. Dent, London, 1975

FELDMAN, Asher. *The Parables and Similes of the Rabbis*. Cambridge University Press, 1924

FELIKS, Jehuda. *Nature and Man in the Bible*. Soncino Press, London, 1981

GINSBERG, Louis. *The Legends of the Jews* (7 vols). Jewish Publication Society of America, Philadelphia, 1947

GORION, Joseph Bin. *Mimekor Ysrael: Classical Jewish Folktales collected by Joseph Bin Gorion*. Indiana University Press, 1976

GUNKEL, Herman. 'The Influence of Babylonian Mythology upon the Creation Story'. In: *Creation in the Old Testament* (ed. Berhard W. Anderson). SPCK, London, 1984

HORTUS SANITATIS. Undated (there were five dated editions between 1490 and 1517). Quoted in SEAGER, 1896

LACHMAN, Ester. 'Birdwatching in Israel'. *The Israel Economist*, Jerusalem, 1983

LUPTON, 1627. 'A Thousand Notable Things of Sundry Sorts: Whereof some are wonderful, some strange, some pleasant, divers necessary, a great sort profitable and many very precious'. Quoted in SEAGER, 1896

PARMELEE, Alice. *All the Birds of the Bible; their stories, identification, and meaning*. Lutterworth Press, London, 1959

SEAGER, H.W. *Natural History in Shakespeare's Time: being extracts illustrative of the Subject as he knew it*. Elliot Stock, London, 1896

TOPSELL, 1607. 'The History of Four-Footed Beasts and Serpents and the Theatre of Insects'. Quoted in SEAGER, 1896

TRISTRAM, H.B. *The Natural History of the Bible*. SPCK, London, 1880

WOOD, J.G. *Bible Animals*. Longmans Green, London, 1869

ZOHARY, Michael. *Plants of the Bible*. Cambridge University Press, 1982